ULTIMATE BIOLOGY -1 : THE CELL AND CELL CYCLE

NCERT BLAST

DR. S.K.VIJAY

Made with ♥ on the Notion Press Platform
www.notionpress.com

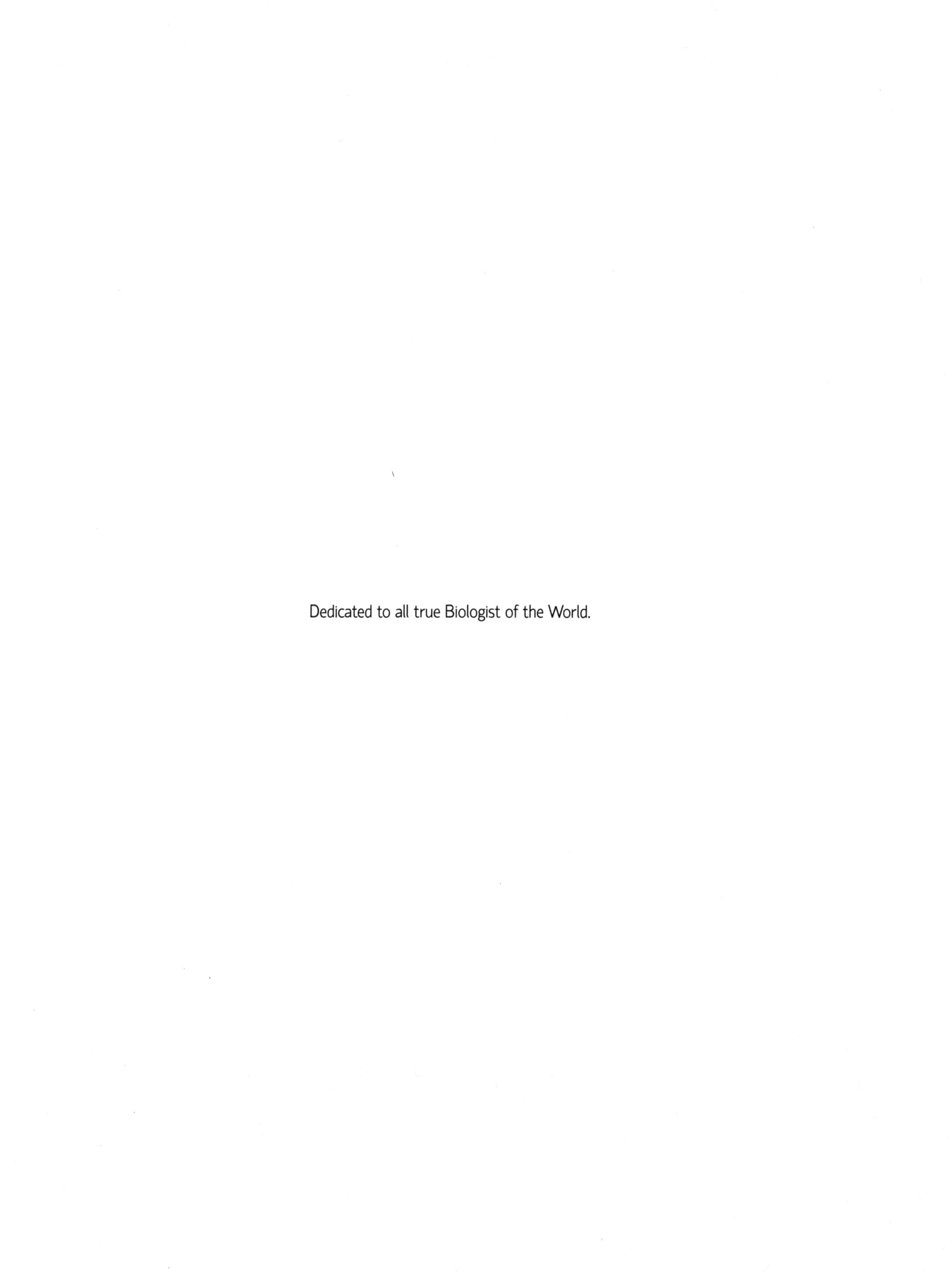

Dedicated to all true Biologist of the World.

Contents

Foreword

Like other subjects , Biology is also a great incredible subject for studets and teachers. This publication is a initial step to explain biology in a small and fast manner. This book is useful to all biology students from 8th to college level and exceltionally inportant to NEET appearing students.

Preface

Keeping in view of 11th, 12th and NEET appearing and other all competitive examinations students , I am presenting this fast revision book. suggestions for improvements will be gratefully acknowledged.

Acknowledgements

I would like to acknowledge the all auther community, my family , colleagues, friends and also my students , who consistently motivate me to write the initial content .

CHAPTER ONE

The Cell : Basic structural and functional unit of an organism

The Cell : Basic structural and functional unit of an organism and cells are the building blocks of the body. The branch of biology which deals cells is called Cytology.

Cell term was given by: Robert Hooke

Cell term was derived from Cella (latin) means Hollow and compartment like, but cell is neither hollow nor compartment like. so we can say that cell is a misnomer term.

Dead Cell was discovered by Robert Hooke in Cork cells(1665). Robert Hooke : English scientist, Book Micrographia

Living cell was discovered by A.V. Leeuwenhoek (1683)

Protoplasm : is the living part of the cell, which comprises of different cellular organelles. It is a jelly-like, colourless, transparent and viscous living substances present within the cell wall.

Protoplasm term was given by : Purkinje

Who called , protoplasm as physical basis of life—Huxley

Protoplast= Plant cell – Cell wall

Types of Cells : Plant cell and Animal Cell

Differences between plant and animal cells- Plastids, Cellwall, Large vacules, plasmodesmata, bigger size, Glyoxysome, centrifugal cytokinesis are the features of plant cell , while animal cells contain centriole, lysosome and showing centripetal cytokinesis.

Types of Cells : Prokaryotic and Eukaryotic Cell

Primtive nucleus, nucleoid, presence of polyamines, Scattered genetic material, single ori, polycistronic mRNA, mesosomes, single envelop system, absence of histone proteins, membrane bound cell organalles, peptidiglycan cell wall, sexual reproduction, zygote, mitosis , meiosis, endocytosis, exocytosis , RNA processing, cytoskeleton are some features of prokaryotic cells .

While with true nucleus and covered genetic material presence of histone, membrane bound cell organalles, mostly cellulosic cellwall, mitosis, meiosis, sexual reproduction, zygote, exocytosis, endocytosis, two envelop system, cytoskeleton, many ori, More A=T, monocistronic mRNA, 9+2 arrangement in cilia and flagella and RNA processing are some features of Eukaryotic cells.

Cell Theory: In 1838, Matthias Schleiden, a German botanist, examined a large number of plants and observed that all plants are composed of different kinds of cells which form the tissues of the plant.

•At about the same time, Theodore Schwann (1839), a British Zoologist, studied different types of animal cells and reported that cells had a thin outer layer which is today known as the ‘plasma membrane’.

•He also concluded, based on his studies on plant tissues, that the presence of cell wall is a unique character of the plant cells. On the basis of this, Schwann proposed the hypothesis that the bodies of animals and plants are composed of cells and products of cells.

•Schleiden and Schwann together formulated the cell theory. This theory however, did not explain as to how new cells were formed.

•Rudolf Virchow (1855) first explained that cells divided and new cells are formed from pre-existing cells (Omnis cellula-e cellula).

•He modified the hypothesis of Schleiden and Schwann to give the cell theory a final shape.

•Cell theory as understood today is:

(i) all living organisms are composed of cells and products of cells.

(ii) all cells arise from pre-existing cells.

•It is the cell theory that emphasised the unity underlying this diversity of forms, i.e., the cellular organisation of all life forms.

Exception of Cell theory: Virus

•Cell theory also created a sense of mystery around living phenomena, i.e., physiological and behavioural processes.

•This mystery was the requirement of integrity of cellular organisation for living phenomena to be demonstrated or observed.

•In studying and understanding the physiological and behavioural processes, one can take a physico-chemical approach and use cell-free systems to investigate. This approach enables us to describe the various processes in molecular terms.

•The approach is established by analysis of living tissues for elements and compounds. It will tell us what types of organic compounds are present in living organisms.

•In the next stage, one can ask the question: What are these compounds doing inside a cell? And, in what way they carry out gross physiological processes like digestion, excretion, memory, defense, recognition, etc.

•In other words we answer the question, what is the molecular basis of all physiological processes? It can also explain the abnormal processes that occur during any diseased condition.

•This physico-chemical approach to study and understand living organisms is called 'Reductionist Biology'.

Properties of Cells :

1. Self organisation 2. Self regulation 3. Self perpetuation 4. Isothermal open system

•What is it that makes an organism living, or what is it that an inanimate thing does not have which a living thing has' ? The answer to this is the presence of the basic unit of life – the cell in all living organisms.

•All organisms are composed of cells. Some are composed of a single cell and are called unicellular organisms while others, like us, composed of many cells, are called multicellular organisms.

•Unicellular organisms are capable of (i) independent existence and (ii) performing the essential functions of life. Anything less than a complete structure of a cell does not ensure independent living.

•Hence, cell is the fundamental structural and functional unit of all living organisms.

•Anton Von Leeuwenhoek first saw and described a live cell.

•Robert Brown later discovered the nucleus.

•G.N. RAMACHANDRAN **(Gopalasamudram Narayanan Ramachandran) :** an outstanding figure in the field of **protein structure,** was the founder of the 'Madras school' of conformational analysis of biopolymers. His discovery of the triple helical structure of collagen published in Nature in 1954 and his analysis of the allowed conformations of proteins through the use of the **'Ramachandran plot'** rank among the most outstanding contributions in structural biology.

•He was born on October 8, 1922, in a small town, not far from Cochin on the southwestern coast of India. His father was a professor of mathematics at a local college and thus had considerable influence in shaping Ramachandran's interest in mathematics.

•After completing his school years, Ramachandran graduated in 1942 as the to ranking student in the B.Sc. (Honors) Physics course of the University of Madras. He received a Ph.D. from Cambridge University in 1949.

•While at Cambridge, Ramachandran met Linus Pauling and was deeply influenced by his publications on models of the α-helix and β-sheet structures that directed his attention to solving the structure of collagen. He passed away at G.N. Ramachandran the age of 78, on April 7, 2001.

•The invention of the microscope and its improvement leading to the electron microscope revealed all the structural details of the cell.

•The cells of the human cheek have an outer membrane as the delimiting structure of the cell. Inside each cell is a dense membrane bound structure called nucleus.

•This nucleus contains the chromosomes which in turn contain the genetic material, DNA.

•Cells that have membrane bound nuclei are called eukaryotic whereas cells that lack a membrane bound nucleus are prokaryotic.

•In both prokaryotic and eukaryotic cells, a semi-fluid matrix called cytoplasm occupies the volume of the cell.

•The cytoplasm is the main arena of cellular activities in both the plant and animal cells. Various chemical reactions occur in it to keep the cell in the 'living state'.

•Besides the nucleus, the eukaryotic cells have other membrane bound distinct structures called organelles like the endoplasmic reticulum (ER), the golgi complex, lysosomes, mitochondria, microbodies and vacuoles.

•The prokaryotic cells lack such membrane bound organelles.

•Ribosomes are non-membrane bound organelles found in all cells – both eukaryotic as well as prokaryotic.

•Within the cell, ribosomes are found not only in the cytoplasm but also within the two organelles – chloroplasts (in plants) and mitochondria and on rough ER.

•Animal cells contain another non-membrane bound organelle called centrosome which helps in cell division.

•Cells differ greatly in size, shape and activities . For example, Mycoplasmas (PPLO- Smallest living cell), the smallest cells, are only 0.3 μm in length while bacteria could be 3 to 5 μm.

•The largest isolated single cell is the egg of an Ostrich.

•Nerve cells are some of the longest cells. Ramie fibres (Plants) : longest plant cell

•Among multicellular organisms, human red blood cells are about 7.0 μm in diameter.

•Cells also vary greatly in their shape. They may be disc-like, polygonal, columnar, cuboid, thread like, or even irregular.

•The shape of the cell may vary with the function they perform.

Cell Shapes :

1. RBC -Round and concave 2. WBC- Amoeboid

3. Columnar Epithellial Cells - Long and narrow 4. Nerve cell- Branched and Long

5. Tracheids- Elongated 6. Mesophyll cell -Rpound and Oval

Cell sizes:

1. Virus- 0.02- 0.2 micrometer 2. PPLO- 0.1- 0.3 micrometer

3. Bacteria- 1-5 micrometer 4. Eukaryotic cell - 10-20 micrometer

5. Human RBC- 7 mircometer

•The prokaryotic cells are represented by bacteria, blue-green algae, mycoplasma and PPLO (Pleuro Pneumonia Like Organisms).

•They are generally smaller and multiply more rapidly than the eukaryotic cells .

•They may vary greatly in shape and size.

•The four basic shapes of bacteria are bacillus (rod like), coccus (spherical), vibrio (comma shaped) and spirillum (spiral).

•The organisation of the prokaryotic cell is fundamentally similar even though prokaryotes exhibit a wide variety of shapes and functions.

•All prokaryotes have a cell wall surrounding the cell membrane except in mycoplasma. The fluid matrix filling the cell is the cytoplasm. There is no well-defined nucleus.

•The genetic material is basically naked, not enveloped by a nuclear membrane. In addition to the genomic DNA (the single chromosome/circular DNA), many bacteria have small circular DNA outside the genomic DNA.

•These smaller DNA are called plasmids. The plasmid DNA confers certain unique phenotypic characters to such bacteria. One such character is resistance to antibiotics. In higher classes you will learn that this plasmid DNA is used to monitor bacterial transformation with foreign DNA.

•Nuclear membrane is found in eukaryotes.

•No organelles, like the ones in eukaryotes, are found in prokaryotic cells except for ribosomes.

•Prokaryotes have something unique in the form of inclusions. A specialised differentiated form of cell membrane called mesosome is the characteristic of prokaryotes (Gram +). They are essentially infoldings of cell membrane.

•Most prokaryotic cells, particularly the bacterial cells, have a chemically complex cell envelope.

•The cell envelope consists of a tightly bound three layered structure i.e., the outermost glycocalyx (sticky) followed by the cell wall and then the plasma membrane.

•Although each layer of the envelope performs distinct function, they act together as a single protective unit.

- Bacteria can be classified into two groups on the basis of the differences in the cell envelopes and the manner in which they respond to the staining procedure developed by Gram viz., those that take up the gram stain are Gram positive and the others that do not are called Gram negative bacteria. **The basis of Gram staining technique is lipid amount in cell wall.**

•Glycocalyx differs in composition and thickness among different bacteria. It could be a loose sheath called the slime layer in some, while in others it may be thick and tough, called the capsule. (allows them to hide fro host immune system)

•The cell wall determines the shape of the cell and provides a strong structural support to prevent the bacterium from bursting or collapsing.

•The plasma membrane is selectively permeable in nature and interacts with the outside world.

•This membrane is similar structurally to that of the eukaryotes.

•A special membranous structure is the mesosome which is formed by the extensions of plasma membrane into the cell. These extensions are in the form of vesicles, tubules and lamellae. They help in cell wall formation, DNA replication and distribution to daughter cells. They also help in respiration, secretion processes, to increase the surface area of the plasma membrane and enzymatic content.

•In some prokaryotes like cyanobacteria, there are other membranous extensions into the cytoplasm called chromatophores which contain pigments.

•Bacterial cells may be motile or non-motile. If motile, they have thin filamentous extensions from their cell wall called flagella.

•Bacteria show a range in the number and arrangement of flagella.

•Bacterial flagellum is composed of three parts – filament, hook and basal body.

•The filament is the longest portion and extends from the cell surface to the outside.

•Besides flagella, Pili and Fimbriae are also surface structures of the bacteria but do not play a role in motility. The pili are elongated tubular structures made of a special protein (Pilin)

•The fimbriae are small bristle like fibres sprouting out of the cell. In some bacteria, they are known to help attach the bacteria to rocks in streams and also to the host tissues.

•**Pili** are long hair like tubular micro-fibres like structures present on the surface of some Gram-negative **bacteria**. They are comparatively shorter than **flagella** and longer than **fimbriae**. (**Fimbriae** are straight and non-helical in nature)

•**Flagella are helical and non-straight in nature.**

•Prokaryotic flagella are made up of flagellin protein while eukaryotic flagella are made up of tubulin.

•Unlike the prokaryotic flagella, eukaryotic flagella have 9+2 arrangement of microtubules.

•Prokaryotic flagella are located outside of the plasma membrane, whereas the flagella in eukaryotes are covered with the plasma membrane.

•In prokaryotes, ribosomes are associated with the plasma membrane of the cell. They are about 15 nm by 20 nm in size and are made of two subunits - 50S and 30S units which when present together form 70S prokaryotic ribosomes.

•Ribosomes are the site of protein synthesis.

•Several ribosomes may attach to a single mRNA and form a chain called polyribosomes or polysome.

•The ribosomes of a polysome translate the mRNA into proteins.

•In eukaryotes, **polyribosomes** are attached to the surface of the rough endoplasmic reticulum and the outer membrane of the nucleus; in bacteria they are **found** free in the cytoplasm.

Eukaryotes: A polyribosome (or polysome or ergosome) is a group of ribosomes bound to an mRNA molecule like "beads" on a "thread".

•**Inclusion bodies:** Reserve material in prokaryotic cells are stored in the cytoplasm in the form of inclusion bodies. These are not bound by any membrane system and lie free in the cytoplasm, e.g., phosphate granules, cyanophycean granules and glycogen granules.

•Gas vacuoles are found in blue green and purple and green photosynthetic bacteria. (for Buoyancy).

- **Cell inclusions are non-living structures present in the cytoplasm of a prokaryotic cell.**
- **The cell inclusions may occur freely inside the cytoplasm (e.g., cyanophycean granules, volutin or phosphate granules, glycogen granules) or**
- **covered by 2-4 nm thick non-lipids, non-unit protein membrane (e.g., gas vacuoles, carboxysomes, sulphur granules, PHB granules).**
- **On the basis of their nature, the cell inclusions are of 3 types - gas vacuoles, inorganic inclusions, and food reserve.**

1.Gas vacuoles - They are gas storing vacuoles found in cyanobacteria, purple and green bacteria and a few other planktonic forms. They protect the bacteria from harmful radiations.

2.Inorganic inclusions - They include volutin granules, sulphur granules, iron granules, magnetic granules, etc. They help the bacteria to orientate themselves along geomagnetic lines (magnetosomes)

3.Food reserve - Blue-green algae have cyanophycean starch, lipid globules, and cyanophycin or protein granules. In bacteria, starch is replaced by glycogen.

•The eukaryotes include all the protists, plants, animals and fungi.

•In eukaryotic cells there is an extensive compartmentalisation of cytoplasm through the presence of membrane bound organelles.

•Eukaryotic cells possess an organised nucleus with a nuclear envelope.

•In addition, eukaryotic cells have a variety of complex locomotory and cytoskeletal structures.

•Their genetic material is organised into chromosomes.

•All eukaryotic cells are not identical.

•Plant and animal cells are different as the former possess cell walls, plastids and a large central vacuole which are absent in animal cells.

•On the other hand, animal cells have centrioles which are absent in almost all plant cells.

Home Work : Fill in the blank

1.It is the ------------------- that emphasised the unity underlying this diversity of forms, i.e., the cellular organisation of all life forms.

2.A description of cell structure and cell growth by ------------- is given in the chapters comprising this unit.

3.Cell theory also created a sense of mystery around living phenomena, i.e., physiological and ------------------------ processes. This mystery was the requirement of integrity of cellular organisation for living phenomena to be demonstrated or observed.

4.This physico-chemical approach to study and understand living organisms is called -------------------- Biology'

5. G.N. RAMACHANDRAN, an outstanding figure in the field of ----------------------------, was the founder of the 'Madras school' of--. His discovery of the triple helical structure of ---------------- published in Nature in 1954 and his analysis of the allowed conformations of proteins through the use of the '-----------------------------' rank among the most outstanding contributions in structural biology.

6. He received a Ph.D. from Cambridge University in 1949. While at Cambridge, Ramachandran met ---------------------and was deeply influenced by his publications on models of the **α-helix and β-sheet** structures that directed his attention to solving the structure of collagen..

7. What is it that makes an organism living, or what is it that an inanimate thing does not have which a living thing has' ? The answer to this is the presence of the basic unit of life – the cell in all living organisms .

8. Unicellular organisms are capable of (i) ----------------------------- and (ii) performing the essential functions of life.

9. Anything less than a complete structure of a cell does not ensure ----------------------------. Hence, cell is the fundamental structural and ------------------------- unit of all living organisms.

10.-------------------------first saw and described a live cell.

11.Robert Brown later discovered the ------------------.

12. In 1838, Malthias Schleiden, a ------------------ botanist, examined a large number of plants and observed that all plants are composed of different kinds of ------------ which form the tissues of the plant.

13.At about the same time, Theodore Schwann (1839), a British ------------------------, studied different types of animal cells and reported that cells had a -------------- outer layer which is today known as the 'plasma membrane'. He also concluded, based on his studies on ------------------tissues, that the presence of cell wall is a unique character of the ------------- cells.

14.On the basis of this, Schwann proposed the hypothesis that the bodies of animals and plants are composed of cells and --------------- of cells.

15.Schleiden and ---------------------- together formulated the cell theory. This theory however, did not explain as to-----------------------------------.

16.------------------------------(1855) first explained that cells divided and new cells are formed from pre-existing cells (------------------------------). He modified the hypothesis of Schleiden and Schwann to give the cell theory a final shape.

17.------------------------------- as understood today is: (i) all living organisms are composed of cells and products of cells. (ii) all cells arise from pre-existing cells.

18. The onion cell which is a typical plant cell, has a distinct cell wall as its outer boundary and just within it is the cell ------------------.

19.The cells of the human cheek have an ----------------membrane as the delimiting structure of the cell.

20.Inside each cell is a dense membrane bound structure called -----------.

21.This nucleus contains the chromosomes which in turn contain the genetic material, --------------.

22.Cells that have membrane bound nuclei are called ------------- whereas cells that lack a membrane bound nucleus are ----------------.

23.In both prokaryotic and eukaryotic cells, a semi-fluid matrix called ----------------- occupies the volume of the cell.

24.The cytoplasm is the main arena of ------------------------------ in both the plant and animal cells. Various chemical reactions occur in it to keep the cell in the 'living state'.

25.Besides the nucleus, the eukaryotic cells have other membrane bound distinct structures called ------------------- like the endoplasmic reticulum (ER), the golgi complex, lysosomes, mitochondria, microbodies and vacuoles. The prokaryotic cells lack such membrane--------------------------.

26.Ribosomes are ------------------------ bound organelles found in all cells – both eukaryotic as well as prokaryotic.

27.Within the cell, ribosomes are found not only in the ----------------------- but also within the two organelles – chloroplasts (in plants) and ----------------- and on rough ER.

28.Animal cells contain another non-membrane bound organelle called ---------------- which helps in cell division.

29. Cells differ greatly in size, shape and activities . For example, ---------------, the smallest cells, are only 0.3 μm in length while bacteria could be 3 to 5 μm.

30.The largest isolated single cell is the egg of an ----------.

31.Among multicellular organisms, human red blood cells are about ---------------- μm in diameter.

32.Nerve cells are some of the ----------- cells. Cells also vary greatly in their shape. They may be disc-like, polygonal, columnar, cuboid, thread like, or even irregular.

33.The shape of the cell may vary with the ------------- they perform.

34.The prokaryotic cells are represented by bacteria, blue-green algae, mycoplasma and PPLO (--).

35.Prokaryotic cells are generally smaller and multiply more rapidly than the -------------------- cells. They may vary greatly in shape and size.

36.The four basic shapes of bacteria are ------------- (rod like), coccus (--------------------), vibrio (--------------- shaped) and spirillum (spiral).

37.The organisation of the prokaryotic cell is fundamentally ------------------- even though prokaryotes exhibit a wide variety of shapes and functions.

38.All prokaryotes have a -----------------surrounding the cell membrane.

39.The fluid matrix filling the cell is the ---------------------.

40.There is no well-defined ---------------------.

41.The genetic material is basically -----------------, not enveloped by a nuclear membrane.

42.In addition to the ----------------------DNA (the single chromosome/circular DNA), many bacteria have small circular DNA outside the genomic DNA. These smaller DNA are called -------------------------.

43.The plasmid DNA confers certain unique -------------------characters to such bacteria. One such character is resistance to antibiotics.

44.The plasmid DNA is used to monitor --------------------------------with foreign DNA.

45.Nuclear membrane is found in --------------------------.

46.No organelles, like the ones in eukaryotes, are found in prokaryotic cells except for -------------------.

47.Prokaryotes have something unique in the form of ----------------------.

48.A specialised differentiated form of cell membrane called---------------- is the characteristic of prokaryotes. They are essentially infoldings of cell membrane.

49. Most prokaryotic cells, particularly the bacterial cells, have a chemically complex ---------------------------------------. The cell envelope consists of a -------------------------------three layered structure i.e., the outermost -------------------followed by the cell wall and then the plasma membrane.

50.Although each layer of the envelope performs ----------------function, they act together as a single --------------------unit.

51.Bacteria can be classified into ---------------groups on the basis of the differences in the cell envelopes and the manner in which they respond to the staining procedure developed by Gram .

52.Those that take up the gram stain are Gram -------------------------------- and the others that do not are called Gram negative bacteria.

53.Glycocalyx differs in composition and ---------------------------- among different bacteria. It could be a loose sheath called the ---------------------------- in some, while in others it may be thick and tough, called the -------------------------------.

54.The cell wall determines the ------------------ of the cell and provides a strong structural support to prevent the bacterium from -----------------------or collapsing.

55.The plasma membrane is semi-permeable in nature and interacts with the ------------- world. This membrane is similar -------------------------------- to that of the eukaryotes.

56.A special membranous structure is the mesosome which is formed by the --------------------------of plasma membrane into the cell. These extensions are in the form of vesicles, tubules and lamellae.

57.-------------------------------- help in cell wall formation, DNA replication and distribution to daughter cells. They also help in respiration, secretion processes, to increase the surface area of the plasma membrane and enzymatic content.

58.In some prokaryotes like cyanobacteria, there are other membranous extensions into the cytoplasm called ---------------------------- which contain pigments.

59.Bacterial cells may be motile or non-motile. If motile, they have thin filamentous extensions from their cell wall called ----------------------.

60.Bacteria show a range in the number and ------------------------- of flagella. Bacterial flagellum is composed of three parts – filament, hook and -----------------body.

61.The filament is the ------------------------- portion and extends from the cell surface to the outside. Besides flagella, Pili and ------------------are also surface structures of the bacteria but do not play a role in motility.

62.The -----------------------------------are elongated tubular structures made of a special protein.

63.The ---------------------------are small bristle like fibres sprouting out of the cell. In some bacteria, they are known to help attach the bacteria to rocks in streams and also to the host tissues.

64. In prokaryotes ribosomes are associated with the ------------------- of the cell.

65. They are about 15 nm by ------- nm in size and are made of two subunits - 50S and ---------S units which when present together form 70S prokaryotic ribosomes.

66. Ribosomes are the site of --------------------- synthesis.

67. Several ribosomes may attach to a single--------------------and form a chain called polyribosomes or polysome.

68. The ribosomes of a polysome----------------------the mRNA into proteins.

69. Reserve material in --------------------cells are stored in the cytoplasm in the form of inclusion bodies.

70. These are not bounded by any membrane system and lie free in the ---------------, e.g., phosphate granules, cyanophycean granules and glycogen granules.

71. Gas vacuoles are found in blue green and---------------------and -------------- photosynthetic bacteria.

72. The eukaryotes include all the protists, plants, animals and fungi. In eukaryotic cells there is an extensive----------------------------------- of cytoplasm through the presence of membrane bound organelles.

73. Eukaryotic cells possess an organised nucleus with a nuclear envelope. In addition, eukaryotic cells have a variety of complex locomotory and cytoskeletal structures. Their genetic material is organised into ----------------------.

74. All eukaryotic cells are not identical. Plant and animal cells are different as the former possess ------------------------, plastids and a large central vacuole which are absent in animal cells.

75. On the other hand, animal cells have ------------------which are absent in almost all plant cells

CHAPTER TWO

Cell Wall

Cell Wall: is a non-living , rigid , very dynamic, malleable structure and capable of broadcasyting signals . It forms an outer covering for the plasma membrane of fungi and plants. Elasticity, tensile strength, adhesion are the properties of the cell wall.

Functions: Cell wall not only gives

1. shape to the cell and protects the cell from mechanical damage and infection,
2. it also helps in cell-to-cell interaction and
3. provides barrier to undesirable macromolecules.

Composition of Cell wall:

1. **Algae** have cell wall, made of cellulose, galactans, mannans and minerals like calcium carbonate, while
2. **Plants :** In other plants it consists of cellulose, hemicellulose, pectins and proteins.
3. **Fungi** : Mostly Chitin
4. **Bacteria :** Peptidoglycan / Mucopeptide/ Murein/ NAG-NAM

- The cell wall of a young plant cell, the primary wall is capable of growth, which gradually diminishes as the cell matures and the secondary wall is formed on the inner (towards membrane) side of the cell.
- The middle lamella (outer most layer of cell wall) is a layer mainly of calcium pectate which holds or glues the different neighbouring cells together and hence called cementing layer. .
- The cell wall and middle lamellae may be traversed by plasmodesmata which connect the cytoplasm of neighbouring cells.
- Fragments of ER and GC (Fragmosomes) form cell plate and this convert in to middle lemella

•A **desmotubule** is an endomembrane derived structure of the plasmodesmata that connects the endoplasmic reticulum of two adjacent plant cells. The **desmotubule** is not actually a tubule, but a compact, cylindrical segment of ER that is found within the larger tubule structure of the plasmodesmata pore.

•**Plasmodesmata** refer to a narrow thread **of** cytoplasm, which passes through the cell walls **of** adjacent plant cells and allows communication **between** them, while **desmotubule** refers to a tube **of** the appressed **endoplasmic reticulum** that runs **between** two adjacent plant cells .

•Plasmodesmata forms living component in the dead cell wall A number of plasmodesmata or cytoplasmic strands are present in pit through which the cytoplasm of one cell is in contact with other. These are lined by plasma membrane and contains a fine tubule called **Desmotubule.**

•ER Play a role in origin of plasmodesmata. These form symplastic system between two cells.

•**Pits** : are relatively thinner portions of the cell wall that adjacent cells can communicate or exchange fluid through. (Unthickned area of secondary cellwall)

•Pits are characteristic of cell walls with secondary layers.

•Generally each pit has a complementary pit opposite of it in the neighboring cell. These complementary pits are called "pit pairs".

•Pits are composed of three parts: the pit chamber, the pit aperture, and the pit membrane.

•The pit chamber is the hollow area where the secondary layers of the cell wall are absent.

•The pit aperture is the opening at either end of the pit chamber. The pit membrane is the primary cell wall and middle lamella, or the membrane between adjacent cell walls, at the middle of the pit chamber.

•The primary cell wall at the pit membrane may also have depressions similar to the pit depressions of the secondary layers. These depressions are primary pit-fields, or primary pits. In the primary pit, the primordial pit provides an interruption in the primary cell wall that the plasmodesmata can cross. The primordial pit is the only aperture in the otherwise continuous primary cell wall.

•Pit pairs are a characteristic feature of xylem, as sap flows through the pits of xylem cells

Types:

•Simple pits: A pit pair in which the diameter of the pit chamber and the diameter of the pit aperture are equal.

•Bordered pits: A pit pair in which the pit chamber is over-arched by the cell wall, creating a larger pit chamber and smaller pit aperture.

•The torus and margo are characteristic features of bordered pit-pairs in gymnosperms, such as Coniferales, *Ginkgo*, and *Gnetales*.

Home work : Fill in the blanks

1. A non-living rigid structure called the cell ------------- forms an outer covering for the plasma membrane of fungi and plants.

2. Cell wall not only gives shape to the cell and ----------------the cell from mechanical damage and infection, it also helps in cell-to-cell interaction and provides barrier to undesirable macromolecules.

3. Algae have cell wall, made of ----------------, galactans, mannans and minerals like calcium carbonate, while in other plants it consists of cellulose, hemicellulose, pectins and proteins.

4. The cell wall of a young plant cell, the ------------------ wall is capable of growth, which gradually diminishes as the cell matures and the secondary wall is formed on the ------------- (towards membrane) side of the cell.

5. The middle lamella is a layer mainly of ---------------- pectate which holds or glues the different neighbouring cells together. The cell wall and middle lamellae may be traversed by --------------- which connect the cytoplasm of neighbouring cells.

CHAPTER THREE

Cell Membrane

Cell Membrane / Plasmamembrane / Plasmalemma : is the membrane found in all cells that separates the interior of the cell from the outside environment. It is selectively or differentially permeable.

- The detailed structure of the membrane was studied only after the advent of the electron microscope in the 1950s. Cell membrane term was given by **Nageli and Kramer.**
- Meanwhile, chemical studies on the cell membrane, especially in human red blood cells (RBCs), enabled the scientists to deduce the possible structure of plasma membrane.
- These studies showed that the cell membrane is mainly composed of **lipids and proteins.**
- The major lipids are **phospholipids (amphipathic)** that are arranged in a bilayer. Also, the lipids are arranged within the membrane with the **polar head (hydrophilic or water loving)** towards the outer sides and the **hydrophobic (water fearing)** tails towards the inner part.
- **This ensures that the nonpolar tail of saturated hydrocarbons is protected from the aqueous environment . Lipid can shows flip-flop movements (rare) .**
- In addition to phospholipids membrane also contains cholesterol.
- Later, biochemical investigation clearly revealed that the cell membranes also possess protein (amphipathic) and carbohydrate.
- The ratio of protein and lipid varies considerably in different cell types.
- **In human beings, the membrane of the erythrocyte has approximately 52 per cent protein and 40 per cent lipids.**
- Depending on the ease of extraction, membrane proteins can be classified as integral or intrinsic (70%) and peripheral or extrinsic (30%).
- Peripheral proteins lie on the surface of membrane while the integral proteins are partially or totally buried in the membrane. **Surface glycoproteins play critically important roles in many cellular events, including cell–cell communications, cell–matrix interactions, and response to environmental cues.**
- An improved model of the structure of cell membrane was proposed by **Singer and Nicolson (1972) widely accepted as fluid mosaic model .**
- According to this, the quasi-fluid nature of lipid enables lateral movement of proteins within the overall bilayer.
- This ability to move within the membrane is measured as its fluidity.
- **Functions of Cell Membrane : The fluid nature of the membrane is also important from the point of view of functions like cell growth, formation of intercellular junctions, secretion, endocytosis, cell division etc.**
- One of the most important functions of the plasma membrane is the transport of the molecules across it.
- The membrane is selectively permeable to some molecules present on either side of it.
- **Cholesterol influences the fluidity of the membrane, and it does so in a bidirectional manner; at high temperatures it decreases fluidity and at low temperatures it increases fluidity**
- The membrane is selectively permeable to some molecules present on either side of it.
- Many molecules can move briefly across the membrane without any requirement of energy and this is called the passive transport.

- Neutral solutes may move across the membrane by the process of simple diffusion along the concentration gradient, i.e., from higher concentration to the lower. Water may also move across this membrane from higher to lower concentration. Movement of water by diffusion is called osmosis.
- As the polar molecules cannot pass through the nonpolar lipid bilayer, they require a carrier protein of the membrane to facilitate their transport across the membrane.
- A few ions or molecules are transported across the membrane against their concentration gradient, i.e., from lower to the higher concentration. Such a transport is an energy dependent process, in which ATP is utilised and is called active transport, e.g., **Na+/K+ Pump.**
- **Bulk transport across the plasma membrane occurs by exocytosis and endocytosis.**

Home work : Fill in the blanks

1. The detailed structure of the membrane was studied only after the advent of the ---------------- microscope in the 1950s.

2. Meanwhile, chemical studies on the cell membrane, especially in human red blood cells (RBCs), enabled the scientists to deduce the possible structure of plasma membrane. These studies showed that the cell membrane is composed of ------------- that are arranged in a bilayer. Also, the lipids are arranged within the membrane with the------------------------------ towards the outer sides and the ------------------- towards the inner part.

3. This ensures that the nonpolar tail of saturated hydrocarbons is protected from the----------------- environment.

4. The lipid component of the membrane mainly consists of ---------------------------.

5. Later, ---------------------------investigation clearly revealed that the cell membranes also possess protein and carbohydrate.

6. The ratio of protein and lipid varies considerably in -------------- cell types.

7. In human beings, the membrane of the erythrocyte has approximately 52 per cent protein and-------- per cent lipids.

8. Depending on the ease of ------------------, membrane proteins can be classified as integral or peripheral.

9. Peripheral proteins lie on the ----------------- of membrane while the integral proteins are partially or totally buried in the membrane.

10. An improved model of the structure of cell membrane was proposed by ---------------------------(1972) widely accepted as fluid mosaic model .

11. According to fluid mosaic model , the quasi-fluid nature of lipid enables ---------------------------movement of proteins within the overall bilayer.

12. This ability to move within the membrane is measured as its ----------------.

13. The --------------- nature of the membane is also important from the point of view of functions like cell growth, formation of intercellular junctions, secretion, endocytosis, cell division etc.

14. One of the most important functions of the plasma membrane is the ----------------of the molecules across it.

15. The membrane is ---------------------permeable to some molecules present on either side of it.

16. Many molecules can move briefly across the membrane without any requirement of energy and this is called the -------------------- transport.

17. Neutral solutes may move across the membrane by the process of ----------------- diffusion along the concentration gradient, i.e., from --------------- concentration to the lower.

18. Water may also move across this membrane from --------------- to ----------------------------------- concentration.

19. Movement of water by diffusion is called -------------------. As the polar molecules cannot pass through the nonpolar ------------------ bilayer, they require a ------------------ protein of the membrane to facilitate their transport across the membrane.

20. A few ions or molecules are transported across the membrane ----------------------- their concentration gradient, i.e., from lower to the higher concentration. Such a transport is an energy dependent process, in which ATP is utilised and is called ------------------- transport, e.g., Na+/K+ Pump.

CHAPTER FOUR

Endomembrane System

EMS : While each of the membranous organelles is distinct in terms of its structure and function, many of these are considered together as an **endomembrane system** because their functions are coordinated.

- The endomembrane system include endoplasmic reticulum (ER), golgi complex, lysosomes and vacuoles.
- Since the functions of the mitochondria, chloroplast and peroxisomes are not coordinated with the above components, these are not considered as part of the endomembrane system.

The endomembrane system includes the nuclear envelope, lysosomes, vesicles, the ER, and Golgi apparatus, as well as the plasma membrane. These cellular components work together to modify, package, tag, and transport proteins and lipids that form the membranes.

The RER modifies proteins and synthesizes phospholipids used in cell membranes. The SER synthesizes carbohydrates, lipids, and steroid hormones; engages in the detoxification of medications and poisons; and stores calcium ions. Sorting, tagging, packaging, and distribution of lipids and proteins take place in the Golgi apparatus. Lysosomes are created by the budding of the membranes of the RER and Golgi. Lysosomes digest macromolecules, recycle worn-out organelles, and destroy pathogens.

Home work : fill in the blanks

1. While each of the membranous organelles is distinct in terms of its structure and function, many of these are considered together as an endomembrane system because their functions are coordinated. The endomembrane system include--------------------------------, golgi complex, lysosomes and ---------------------.

2. Since the ------------------------ of the mitochondria, chloroplast and peroxisomes are not coordinated with the above components, these are not considered as part of the endomembrane system.

CHAPTER FIVE

Endoplasmic Reticulum

ER: Endoplasmic reticulum : Biosynthetic factory : within cytoplasm + little net. ER tem was proposed by **Porter.**

Composition of ER: 1. Cisternae 2., Tubules 3. Vesicles

Electron microscopic studies of eukaryotic cells reveal the presence of a network or reticulum of tiny tubular structures scattered in the cytoplasm that is called the endoplasmic reticulum (ER) .

Hence, ER divides the intracellular space into two distinct compartments, i.e., luminal (inside ER) and extra luminal (cytoplasm) compartments.

•The ER often shows ribosomes attached to their outer surface.

Types of ER: 1. Rough ER 2. Smooth ER

•The endoplasmic reticulum bearing ribosomes on their surface is called rough endoplasmic reticulum (RER).

•In the absence of ribosomes they appear smooth and are called smooth endoplasmic reticulum (SER).

•RER is frequently observed in the cells actively involved in protein synthesis and secretion. In addition to making secretary proteins , it is a membrane factory for the cell. (it grows in place by adding membrane proteins and phospholipids to its own membrane.)

•They are extensive and continuous with the outer membrane of the nucleus.

•The smooth endoplasmic reticulum is the major site for synthesis of lipid.

•In animal cells lipid-like steroidal hormones are synthesised in SER. , metabolism of carbohydrates, detoxification of drugs and poisons, muscle contraction and release and uptake / storage of calcium ions.

•Cytochrome P 450 is associated with SER and is involved in breakdown of foreign compounds (Xenobiotics)

•With the help of Ribophorin (Glyco protein) , ribosome(60S subunit unit) is attached with RER.

- ER of Nerve Cell : Nissl's Body
- ER of Skeltal and Cardiac Muscles : T- tubules
- ER of Retina : Myeloid Body

Home work : Fill in the blanks

1.---------------------------------studies of eukaryotic cells reveal the presence of a network or reticulum of tiny tubular structures scattered in the cytoplasm that is called the endoplasmic reticulum (ER).

2. Hence, ER divides the intracellular space into two distinct compartments, i.e., ------------------ (inside ER) and extra luminal (cytoplasm) compartments.

3. The ER often shows ribosomes attached to their outer surface.

4. The endoplasmic reticulun bearing ribosomes on their surface is called ----------------- endoplasmic reticulum (RER).

5. In the ----------------of ribosomes they appear smooth and are called smooth endoplasmic reticulum (SER).

6. RER is frequently observed in the cells actively involved in-- and secretion.

9. . They are extensive and continuous with the---------------------membrane of the nucleus.

10. The ------------------ endoplasmic reticulum is the major site for synthesis of lipid. In animal cells lipid-like steroidal hormones are synthesised in ---------ER.

CHAPTER SIX

Golgi Body

Golgi complex : Receiving and Shipping Center, Lipchondria, Appráto reticulare, Dalton complex, Dictyosome in Plants, Baker's Body

•Camillo Golgi (1898) first observed densely stained reticular structures near the nucleus.

Components: 1. Cisternae 2. Tubules 3. Vesicles

•These were later named Golgi bodies after him. They consist of many flat, disc-shaped sacs or cisternae of 0.5µm to 1.0µm diameter .

•These are stacked parallel to each other. In plants and invertibrates GC is diffused in the cell while in vertibratesGc is situated above nucleus.

•Varied number of cisternae are present in a Golgi complex.

•The Golgi cisternae are concentrically arranged near the nucleus with distinct convex cis or the forming face/ F-face/ proximal face and concave trans or the maturing face or M-face or Distal face.

•The cis and the trans faces of the organelle are entirely different, but **interconnected in animal cells , while in plant cells – unconnected.**

•The golgi apparatus principally performs the function of **packaging materials**, to be delivered either to the intra-cellular targets or secreted outside the cell.

•Materials to be packaged in the form of vesicles from the ER fuse with the cis face of the golgi apparatus and move towards the maturing face. This explains, why the golgi apparatus remains in close association with the endoplasmic reticulum.

•A number of proteins synthesised by ribosomes on the endoplasmic reticulum are modified in the cisternae of the golgi apparatus before they are released from its trans face.

- Golgi apparatus is the important site of formation of glycoproteins and glycolipids.(glycosylation of lipid and proteins)
- other functions of GC: Lysosome formation , acrosome formation, secretion of tears, saliva , mucus.

Home work : Fill in the blanks

1. Camillo Golgi (--------------------) first observed --------------------stained reticular structures near the -------------------. These were later named Golgi bodies after him.

2. They consist of many flat, disc-shaped sacs or cisternae of 0.5µm to -----------------µm diameter . These are stacked ------------------ to each other.

3. Varied number of ---------------- are present in a Golgi complex.

4. The Golgi cisternae are---------------------------- arranged near the nucleus with distinct convex cis or the forming face and concave trans or the -------------- face.

5. The cis and the trans faces of the organelle are entirely----------------, but interconnected.

6. The golgi apparatus principally performs the function of ------------------------------ materials, to be delivered either to the --------------------cellular targets or secreted outside the cell.

7. Materials to be packaged in the form of vesicles from the ER fuse with the cis face of the golgi apparatus and move towards the ---------------face. This explains, why the golgi apparatus remains in close association with the

endoplasmic reticulum.

8. A number of proteins synthesised by ribosomes on the endoplasmic reticulum are------------------------in the cisternae of the golgi apparatus before they are released from its -------------------- face.

9. --------------------------------- is the important site of formation of glycoproteins and glycolipids.

10. Lysosome formation occurs by ------------------------.

CHAPTER SEVEN

Lysosome and Vacuole

- Lysosomes: Digestive compartment : These are membrane bound vesicular structures formed by the process of packaging in the golgi apparatus.
- It is also called as Recycling center, Suicidal bad, Disposal unit.
- It was discovered by C.De Duve
- The isolated lysosomal vesicles have been found to be very rich in almost all types of hydrolytic enzymes (hydrolases – lipases, proteases, carbohydrases) optimally active at the acidic pH (4-5).
- These enzymes are capable of digesting carbohydrates, proteins, lipids and nucleic acids.
- It is single membrane bound structure and a special property is present in the lysosomal membrane that is attaches easily by other membranes.
- Two types of chemicals present on lysosomal membranes : 1. labilisers (destabilisers) - Vitamin A, D, E , K, progesterone, testosterone 2. Stabilisers : Heparin cortisone, cholesterol
- Lysosomal enzymes only release after rupturing of lysosome, hence called suicidal bag.
- In Lysosome polymorphism is present , it means it covert in to different forms like primary, secondary and tertiary.
- Types of Lysosome: 1. Primary lysosome (formed by GC) 2. Secondary lysosome : it may be heterophagosome or autophagosome or residual body(telolysosome)
- Functions of lysosome: 1. digestion 2. Cause mutation (bursting of lysosome before time cause mutation due to presence of DNAase. 3. Metamorphosis of tadpole tail is due to catapsin. 4. recycling of wornout cells (autophagy) 5. Uterus regrassion 6. Defence 7. Help in fertilization
- Some of the most common lysosomal storage disorders include:

•**Gaucher disease:** Gaucher disease often causes spleen and liver enlargement, blood problems and bone issues.

•**Fabry disease:** This disorder often causes severe burning pains in hands and feet and, in some cases, a distinctive skin rash on the legs.

•**Niemann-Pick disease:** Similar to Gaucher disease, Niemann-Pick disease involves organ enlargement, lung dysfunction and central nervous system damage.

•**Hunter syndrome:** This disease is part of a group of disorders that cause bone and joint deformity as well as interference with normal growth.

•**Glycogen storage disease II (Pompe disease):** Pompe disease may cause heart enlargement and heart failure in infants. It may also cause respiratory problems and severe muscle weakness in adults.

•**Tay-Sachs disease:** This disorder causes severe and fatal mental and physical deterioration, with both an early-onset and a late-onset form.

Vacuoles : The vacuole is the membrane-bound space found in the cytoplasm.

•It contains water, sap, excretory product and other materials not useful for the cell.

•The vacuole is bound by a single membrane called tonoplast. In plant cells the vacuoles can occupy up to 90 per cent of the volume of the cell.

•In plants, the tonoplast facilitates the transport of a number of ions and other materials against concentration gradients into the vacuole, hence their concentration is significantly higher in the vacuole than in the cytoplasm.

•In Amoeba the contractile vacuole is important for osmoregulation and excretion.

•In many cells, as in protists, food vacuoles are formed by engulfing the food particles.

Home work : Fill in the blanks

1. ------------------ are membrane bound vesicular structures formed by the process of packaging in the golgi apparatus.

2. The isolated lysosomal vesicles have been found to be very rich in almost all types of -------------------- enzymes (hydrolases – lipases, proteases, carbohydrases) optimally active at the----------------pH. These enzymes are capable of digesting carbohydrates, proteins, lipids and nucleic acids.

3. The vacuole is the membrane- ------------------ found in the cytoplasm. It contains ------------------, sap, excretory product and other materials not useful for the cell.

4. The vacuole is bound by a ------------------- membrane called -----------------------------------.

5. In plant cells the vacuoles can occupy up to-------------------------per cent of the volume of the cell.

6. In plants, the tonoplast facilitates the transport of a number of ions and other materials -------------------------- concentration gradients into the vacuole, hence their concentration is significantly ---------------- in the vacuole than in the cytoplasm.

7. In Amoeba the contractile vacuole is important for -------------------------.

8. In many cells, as in -----------------, food vacuoles are formed by engulfing the food particles

9. pH of lusosomal enzymes is ----------------

10. Autophagy is the function of --------------.

CHAPTER EIGHT

Mitochondria

Mitochondria (sing.: mitochondrion), unless specifically stained, are not easily visible under the microscope. It is also called as chondriosome, power house of the cell, plastochondria, oxidosome, cellular furnace.

- The number of mitochondria per cell is variable depending on the physiological activity of the cells. More numner found in metabolically active cells. In Flight muscles cells of birds , 5 laks mitochondria present.
- In terms of shape and size also, considerable degree of variability is observed.
- Typically it is sausage-shaped or cylindrical having a diameter of 0.2-1.0μm (average 0.5μm) and length 1.0-4.1μm.
- Each mitochondrion is a double membrane-bound structure with the outer membrane and the inner membrane dividing its lumen distinctly into two aqueous compartments, i.e., the outer compartment and the inner compartment.
- The inner compartment is filled with a dense homogeneous substance called the matrix. The outer membrane forms the continuous limiting boundary of the organelle.
- The inner membrane forms a number of infoldings called the cristae (sing.: crista) towards the matrix . on the inner side of the inner membrane of the cristae, **oxysomes or FM particles or Recker's particles are present**, where oxidative phosphorylation occurs.
- The cristae increase the surface area. The two membranes have their own specific enzymes associated with the mitochondrial function.
- Mitochondria are the sites of aerobic respiration.
- They produce cellular energy in the form of ATP, hence they are called 'power houses' of the cell. It store divalent cations ($Ca2+$ and $Mg2+$)
- The matrix also possesses **single circular DNA molecule**, a few RNA molecules, **ribosomes (70S)** and the components required for the synthesis of proteins. Hence called Semiautonomous organallae
- Origin : endosymbiotic
- The mitochondria divide by fission and staining by Janus green B

Home work : Fill in the blanks

1. Mitochondria (sing.: mitochondrion), unless ------------------ stained, are not easily visible under the microscope.

2. The number of mitochondria per cell is-------------------- depending on the physiological activity of the cells. In terms of shape and size also, considerable degree of variability is observed. Typically it is ---------------------shaped or cylindrical having a diameter of 0.2-1.0μm (average 0.5μm) and length 1.0-------μm.

3. Each mitochondrion is a-------------- membrane-bound structure with the outer membrane and the inner membrane dividing its lumen distinctly into two aqueous compartments, i.e., the outer compartment and the inner compartment.

4. The inner compartment is called the ------------------. The outer membrane forms the ------------------ limiting boundary of the organelle.

5. The inner membrane forms a number of ------------------ called the cristae (sing.: crista) towards the matrix .

6. The cristae --------------------- the surface area.

7. The two membranes have their own specific enzymes associated with the mitochondrial function. Mitochondria are the sites of ---------------------- respiration. They produce cellular energy in the form of ----------- hence they are called '-----------------------------' of the cell.

8. The matrix also possesses ----------------------------- circular DNA molecule, a few RNA molecules, ribosomes (----S) and the components required for the synthesis of proteins.

9. The mitochondria divide by ---.

10. Cardiolipin (lipoprotein) present in inner membrane of ----------------------.

CHAPTER NINE

Plastid

Plastids term was given by Haeckel . Plastids are found in all plant cells and in euglenoides.

- These are easily observed under the microscope as they are large. They bear some specific pigments, thus imparting specific colours to the plants.
- Based on the type of pigments plastids can be classified into **chloroplasts, chromoplasts and leucoplasts.** All these plastids are interconvertible.
- The chloroplasts contain chlorophyll and carotenoid pigments which are responsible for trapping light energy essential for photosynthesis.
- In the chromoplasts **fat soluble carotenoid pigments like carotene, xanthophylls** and others are present. This gives the part of the plant a yellow, orange or red colour.
- The leucoplasts are the colourless plastids of varied shapes and sizes with stored nutrients:
- **Aleuroplast** store proteins e.g. Maize
- **Amyloplasts** store carbohydrates (starch), e.g., potato;
- **elaioplasts** store oils and fats whereas the aleuroplasts store proteins.
- **Etioplast** (Fatty acid): when a plant is kapt in dark for a long time , etioplast are developed. Here plants become yellow. The phenomena is called etiolation.

•Majority of the chloroplasts of the green plants are found in the mesophyll cells of the leaves. These are lens-shaped, oval, spherical, discoid or even ribbon-like organelles having variable length (5-10μm) and width (2-4μm).

•Their number varies from 1 per cell of the Chlamydomonas, a green alga to 20-40 per cell in the mesophyll. Like mitochondria, the chloroplasts are also double membrane bound. Of the two, the **inner chloroplast membrane is relatively less permeable**. Porins present on outer membrane.

•The space limited by the inner membrane of the chloroplast is called the stroma. A number of organised **flattened membranous sacs called the thylakoids,** are present in the stroma.

•Thylakoids are arranged in stacks like the piles of coins called grana (singular: granum) or the intergranal thylakoids. In addition, there are **flat membraneous tubules called the stroma lamellae (fret channel)** connecting the thylakoids of the different grana.

•The membrane of the thylakoids enclose a space called a lumen. The stroma of the chloroplast contains enzymes required for the synthesis of **carbohydrates and proteins.** It also contains small, double stranded circular DNA molecules and ribosomes.

•Chlorophyll pigments are present in the thylakoids. The ribosomes of the chloroplasts are smaller (70S) than the cytoplasmic ribosomes (80S).

•In Chloroplast **photophosphorylation** takes place while in mitochondria **oxidative phosphorylation** takes place.

Home Work: Fill in the blanks

1. Plastids are found in all plant cells and in -------------------------.
2. These are easily observed under the microscope as they are --------------.
3. They bear some specific pigments, thus imparting specific colours to the plants. Based on the type of pigments plastids can be classified into chloroplasts, chromoplasts and ----------------------------------.

4. The --------------------------- contain chlorophyll and carotenoid pigments which are responsible for trapping light energy essential for photosynthesis.

5. In the chromoplasts -------------------------soluble carotenoid pigments like carotene, xanthophylls and others are present. This gives the part of the plant a yellow, orange or red colour.

6. The leucoplasts are the ---------plastids of varied shapes and sizes with stored nutrients:

7. Amyloplasts store ------------------------(starch), e.g., potato;

8. elaioplasts store -------------------------and fats .

9. The aleuroplasts store ------------------------------.

10. Majority of the chloroplasts of the green plants are found in the -------------------cells of the leaves.

11. These are lens-shaped, oval, spherical, discoid or even ribbon-like organelles having variable length (--------------------mm) and width (2-4mm).

12. Their number varies from --------------- per cell of the Chlamydomonas, a green alga to 20-40 per cell in the ----------------------------.

13. Like mitochondria, the chloroplasts are also --------------- membrane bound. Of the two, the inner chloroplast membrane is relatively ----------------- permeable.

14. The space limited by the inner membrane of the chloroplast is called the -----------------------.

15. A number of organised flattened membranous sacs called the ------------------------------, are present in the stroma .

16. ---------------------------are arranged in stacks like the piles of coins called grana (singular: granum) or the intergranal thylakoids.

17. In addition, there are flat membranous ------------------------- called the stroma lamellae connecting the thylakoids of the different grana.

18. The membrane of the thylakoids enclose a space called a --------------------------.

19. The stroma of the chloroplast contains enzymes required for the synthesis of ---------------------and proteins.

20. It also contains small, double-stranded --------------------- DNA molecules and ribosomes. Chlorophyll pigments are present in the --------------------------------. The ribosomes of the chloroplasts are smaller (70S) than the -------------------------- ribosomes (80S).

CHAPTER TEN

Ribosome

Ribosomes (Palade granules) are the granular structures first observed under the electron microscope as dense particles by George Palade (1953). It is also called as protein factory, work bench of protein, organalle with in organalle.

- They are composed of ribonucleic acid (RNA) and proteins and are not surrounded by any membrane.
- The eukaryotic ribosomes are 80S while the prokaryotic ribosomes are 70S.
- Each ribosome has two subunits, larger and smaller subunits .
- The two subunits of 80S ribosomes are 60S and 40S while that of 70S ribosomes are 50S and 30S. Here 'S' (Svedberg's Unit) stands for the sedimentation coefficient; it is indirectly a measure of density and size. Both 70S and 80S ribosomes are composed of two subunits. These subunits are united by Mg ions.

Home work : Fill in the blanks

1. Ribosomes are the granular structures first observed under the electron microscope as dense particles by ----------------------- (1953).
2. They are composed of ---------------------and proteins and are not surrounded by any membrane.
3. The eukaryotic ribosomes are 80S while the --------------------- ribosomes are 70S.
4. Here 'S' stands for the sedimentation coefficient; it indirectly is a measure of ------------------ and size.
5. Both 70S and 80S ribosomes are composed of two -------------------------.

CHAPTER ELEVEN

Cytoskeleton

Cytoskeleton : (MT (Plants and animals) + MF (Plants and animals) + Ifs – only in some animals)

An elaborate network of filamentous proteinaceous structures consisting of microtubules (Actin and Myosin) , microfilaments (tubulin) and intermediate filaments present in the cytoplasm is collectively referred to as the cytoskeleton. it is absent in prokaryotes.

The cytoskeleton in a cell are involved in many functions such as **mechanical support, motility, maintenance of the shape of the cell.**

Of the three types of protein fibers in the cytoskeleton, **microfilaments** are the narrowest. They have a **diameter** of about 6-7 nm and are made up of many linked monomers of a protein called actin.

Home work : Fill in the blanks

1. An elaborate network of filamentous proteinaceous structures consisting of microtubules, microfilaments and intermediate filaments present in the cytoplasm is collectively referred to as the -------------------.

2. The cytoskeleton in a cell are involved in many functions such as mechanical support, motility, ----------------- of the shape of the cell.

CHAPTER TWELVE

Centriole

Centrosome : is an organelle usually containing two cylindrical structures called centrioles. Centrosome was discovered by T. Bovary and it is a membrane less structure.

•They are surrounded by amorphous pericentriolar materials. Both the centrioles in a centrosome lie perpendicular to each other in which each has an organisation like the **cartwheel.**

•They are made up of **nine evenly spaced** peripheral fibrils of tubulin protein with an angle of 40 degree.

•Each of the **peripheral fibril is a triplet.**

The adjacent triplets are also linked by A-C linker. . The central part of the proximal region of the centriole is also proteinaceous and called the hub, which is connected with tubules of the peripheral triplets by **radial spokes** made of protein.

- The centrioles form the basal body of cilia or flagella, and spindle fibres that give rise to spindle apparatus during cell division in animal cells.

Home Work : Fill in the blanks

1, ------------------- is an organelle usually containing two -----------------structures called centrioles. They are surrounded by amorphous-------------------- materials.

2. Both the centrioles in a centrosome lie ---------------------to each other in which each has an organisation like the --------------------.

3 They are made up of--------------- evenly spaced peripheral fibrils of --------------. Each of the peripheral fibril is a --------------------.

4. The adjacent triplets are also linked. The central part of the centriole is also ------------------------ and called the hub, which is connected with tubules of the peripheral triplets by radial spokes made of ---------.

5.The centrioles form the ------------- of cilia or flagella, and spindle fibres that give rise to spindle apparatus during cell division in animal cells.

CHAPTER THIRTEEN

Cilia and Flagella

Cilia (sing.: cilium) and flagella (sing.: flagellum) are hair-like outgrowths of the cell membrane.

- Cilia are small structures which work like oars, causing the movement of either the cell or the surrounding fluid.
- Flagella are comparatively longer and responsible for cell movement.

•The prokaryotic bacteria also possess flagella but these are structurally different from that of the eukaryotic flagella.

•The electron microscopic study of a cilium or the flagellum show that they are covered with plasma membrane.

•Their core called the **axoneme,** possesses a number of microtubules running parallel to the long axis.

•The axoneme usually has nine doublets of radially arranged peripheral microtubules, and a pair of centrally located microtubules.

- **Such an arrangement of axonemal microtubules is referred to as the 9+2 array** .

•The central tubules are connected by bridges and is also enclosed by a central sheath, which is connected to one of the tubules of each **peripheral doublets by a radial spoke with an angle of 10 degree.**

•Thus, there are nine radial spokes. The peripheral doublets are also interconnected by linkers (A-B linkers).

•Both the cilium and flagellum emerge from centriole-like structure called the basal bodies.

Home work : Fill in the blanks

1. Cilia (sing.: cilium) and flagella (sing.: flagellum) are hair-like outgrowths of the -----------------------------.
2. Cilia are small structures which work like ------------------, causing the movement of either the cell or the surrounding fluid.
3. Flagella are comparatively longer and responsible for ---.
4. The prokaryotic bacteria also possess flagella but these are --------------------------------- different from that of the eukaryotic flagella.
5. The electron microscopic study of a cilium or the flagellum show that they are covered with -----------------------.
6. Their core called the -------------------------, possesses a number of microtubules running parallel to the ---------------axis.
7. The axoneme usually has --------------------- of doublets of radially arranged peripheral microtubules, and a pair of ----------------------------- located microtubules. Such an arrangement of axonemal microtubules is referred to as the 9+2 array .
8. The central tubules are connected by bridges and is also enclosed by a central sheath, which is connected to one of the tubules of each peripheral doublets by a------------------------. Thus, there are ------------------- radial spokes.
9. The peripheral doublets are also-----------------------by linkers.
10. Both the cilium and flagellum emerge from centriole-like structure called the ----------------------------.

CHAPTER FOURTEEN

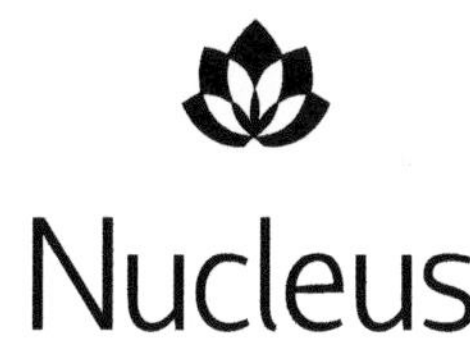

Nucleus

•Nucleus as a cell organelle was first described by Robert Brown as early as 1831 in orchid root cell. .

•Later the material of the nucleus stained by the basic dyes was given the name chromatin by Flemming.

- The interphase nucleus (nucleus of a cell when it is not dividing) has highly extended and elaborate nucleoprotein fibres called chromatin, nuclear matrix and one or more spherical bodies called nucleoli (sing.: nucleolus).

•Electron microscopy has revealed that the nuclear envelope, which consists of two parallel membranes with a space between (10 to 50 nm) called the perinuclear space, forms a barrier between the materials present inside the nucleus and that of the cytoplasm.

•The outer membrane usually remains continuous with the endoplasmic reticulum and also bears ribosomes on it. At a number of places the nuclear envelope is interrupted by minute pores, which are formed by the fusion of its two membranes.

•These nuclear pores are the passages through which movement of **RNA and protein** molecules takes place in both directions between the nucleus and the cytoplasm.

•Normally, there is only one nucleus per cell, variations in the number of nuclei are also frequently observed.

•Can you recollect names of organisms that have more than one nucleus per cell?

- **Some mature cells even lack nucleus, e.g., erythrocytes of many mammals and sieve tube cells of vascular plants.**
- **Coenocytic cells : Aseptate multinucleate condition e.g. Albugo , Voucheria**
- **Syncytium : multinucleate condition arise due to free nuclear divisions e.g. Ascahelminthes, Coconut .**

•Would you consider these cells as 'living'? The nuclear matrix or the nucleoplasm contains nucleolus and chromatin.

•The nucleoli are spherical structures present in the nucleoplasm. The content of nucleolus is continuous with the rest of the nucleoplasm as it is not a membrane bound structure.

•It is a site for active ribosomal RNA synthesis.

•Larger and more numerous nucleoli are present in cells actively carrying out protein synthesis.

•Each **chromosome** is divided into two sections (**arms**) based on the location of a narrowing (constriction) called the centromere. By convention, the shorter **arm** is called **p**, and the longer **arm** is called **q. (P means – petite or small)**

•Arm ratio: q/p- This is expressed with the **ratio** "long **arm** to short **arm**".

•In human five chromosomes (5 pairs) are known as satellite chromosomes – 13, 14, 15, 21, 22

•Telomere: ends of chromosome : sealing of ends. Or prevent chromosome loss.

•Euchromatin: loosely coiled, active. And Heterochromatin: Densely packed , inactive

•You may recall that the interphase nucleus has a loose and indistinct network of nucleoprotein fibres called chromatin.

•But during different stages of cell division, cells show structured chromosomes in place of the nucleus.

•Chromatin contains DNA and some basic proteins called histones, some non-histone proteins and also RNA.

•A single human cell has approximately two metre long thread of DNA distributed among its 46 (twenty three pairs) chromosomes.

•A typical human cell has 46 chromosome in its nucleus, the exceptions are human sex cells (egg and sperm) which as only 23 chromosome.

•Every chromosome (visible only in dividing cells) essentially has a primary constriction or the centromere on the sides of which disc shaped structures called kinetochores are present .

•Centromere holds two chromatids of a chromosome.

•Based on the position of the centromere, the chromosomes can be classified into four types

•The metacentric chromosome has middle centromere forming two equal arms of the chromosome.

•The sub-metacentric chromosome has centromere slightly away from the middle of the chromosome resulting into one shorter arm and one longer arm.

•In case of acrocentric chromosome the centromere is situated close to its end forming one extremely short and one very long arm, whereas the telocentric chromosome has a terminal centromere.

•Sometimes a few chromosomes have non-staining secondary constrictions at a constant location. This gives the appearance of a small fragment called the satellite.

•Diagramatic representation of Karyotype- Idiogram

•Informosomes – m RNA + Protein : use in development of embryo (lampbrush)

Home work : fill in the blanks

1. Nucleus as a cell organelle was first described by -------------------- as early as 1831.

2. Later the material of the nucleus stained by the-------------- dyes was given the name chromatin by -------.

3. The interphase nucleus (nucleus of a cell when it is not dividing) has highly extended and elaborate nucleoprotein fibres called ---------------------------, nuclear matrix and one or more spherical bodies called nucleoli (sing.: nucleolus)

4.Electron microscopy has revealed that the nuclear envelope, which consists of two parallel membranes with a space between (-----------------------nm) called the perinuclear space, forms a barrier between the materials present inside the nucleus and that of the cytoplasm.

5. The outer membrane usually remains continuous with the ------------------------------and also bears ribosomes on it.

6. At a number of places the nuclear envelope is interrupted by minute pores, which are formed by the----------------- of its two membranes.

7. hese nuclear pores are the passages through which movement of -------------------and protein molecules takes place in both directions between the nucleus and the cytoplasm.

8. Normally, there is only one nucleus per cell, variations in the number of nuclei are also frequently observed.

9. Organisms that have more than one nucleus per cell?--

10. Some mature cells even ----------------- nucleus, e.g., erythrocytes of many mammals and sieve tube cells of vascular plants.

11. The nuclear matrix or the nucleoplasm contains nucleolus and -----------------------

12. The nucleoli are spherical structures present in the ------------------------.

13. The content of nucleolus is continuous with the rest of the nucleoplasm as it is not a ---------------------------------------structure.

14. It is a site for ------------------------------------RNA synthesis.

15. ----------------------------------and more numerous nucleoli are present in cells actively carrying out protein synthesis.

16. The interphase nucleus has a ----------------------- and indistinct network of nucleoprotein fibres called chromatin.

17. But during different stages of cell division, cells show structured chromosomes in place of the -------------------.

18. Chromatin contains DNA and some basic proteins called -----------------, some ----------------------proteins and also RNA.

19. A single human cell has approximately------------------ metre long thread of DNA distributed among its forty six (twenty three pairs) chromosomes.

20. Every chromosome essentially has a ------------------ constriction or the centromere on the sides of which disc shaped structures called -----------------------are present .

21. Based on the ------------------------ of the centromere, the chromosomes can be classified into four types.

22. The --------------------- chromosome has middle centromere forming two equal arms of the chromosome.

23. The sub-metacentric chromosome has centromere nearer to one end of the chromosome resulting into one ------------------arm and one longer arm.

24. In case of ---------------------------chromosome the centromere is situated close to its end forming one extremely short and one very long arm, whereas the ----------------------- chromosome has a terminal centromere.

25. Sometimes a few chromosomes have -------------------------secondary constrictions at a constant location. This gives the appearance of a small fragment called the ---.

CHAPTER FIFTEEN

Microbodies

Glyoxysome: discovered by Tolberts and Beevers.

It is single membrane bound structure .

Origin – From ER , Contain enzymes of Glyxoylate cycle. Through which fat convert in to carbohydrates-Gluconeogenesis. Found in germinating seeds(Fatty) -Castor, Groundnut) .

Absent in animals.

Spherosome: Discovered by Perner.

It is Unit membrane bound structure. It Take part in storage and synthesis of fats. Found in endosperm cells of oily seeds.

Contain Hydrolytic enzymes and also considered as plant lysosome They are produced by SER

Peroxysomes : also called Uricosomes and was discovered by de Duve.

Peroxydases enzymes (Oxidases and catalases) are abundantly present , hence called peroxysome.

Peroxysome in the liver detoxify alcohol and other harmful compounds.

CHAPTER SIXTEEN

Nonliving Inclusions

Nonliving Inclusions:

1. CaCO3 Crystals: Cystolyth (lithocyte)- Ficus

2. Calcium Oxalate Crystals: Raphides(Lemna and Pistia) and Group of Raphide- Druces(Colocasia)

3. Silica Crystals: Grasses

Home Work : Fill in the blanks

1. ________________ is the fundamental strcutural and functional unit of all living organism.
2. ________________ first saw and described a live cell and ________________ discovered the nucleus.
3. ________________ and ________________ together formulated the cell theory.
4. 'Omnis cellula-e-cellula' was explained by ________________ .
5. Cells that have membrane bound nuclei are called ________________ whereas cells that lack a membrane bound nucleus are called ________________ .
6. ________________ are non-membrane bound organelles found in ALL cells.
7. The smallest cell is ________________ of ______μm in length.
8. The four basic shapes of bacteria are bacillus (rod like), coccus (spherical), ________________ (comma shaped) and ________________ (spiral).
9. A typical eukaryotic cell is of 10-20μm, PPLO ______μm and that of viruses is ______μm.
10. Many bacteria have small circular DNA in addition to genomic DNA and is called ________________ .
11. In bacteria, the infolding of cell membrane is called ________________, which is the charateristic of prokaryotes.
12. The cell envelope of prokaryotic cell consist of three layer - ________________ , ________________ and ________________ .
13. In some prokaryotes, glycocalyx could be loose sheath called ________________ and in sometime it may be thick and tough called ________________ .
14. In bacteria, ________________ determines the shape of cell and provides structural support.
15. In cyanobacteria, the membranous extensions into cytoplasm called ________________ contains pigments.
16. Motile bacteria have thin filamentous extension from their cell wall called ________________ , which is composed of three parts ________________ , ______________ and basal body. ________________ is the longest portion and extend from cell surface to the outside.
17. Surface structure present in bacteria are flagella, ________________ and ________________ .
18. Ribosome are about ________________ size and are made up of two subunits- ___________ and________________, which form ________________ prokaryotic ribosome.
19. Several ribosome may attach to a single mRNA and form a chain called ________________ .
20. Reserve material in prokaryotic cells are stored in cytoplasm in the form of ________________ .
21. The cell membrane is composed of ________________ that are arranged in a ________________ .
22. In humans, the membrane of the erythrocyte has approximately __________% protein and __________% lipids.
23. According to ________________ model, the quasi-fluid nature of lipid enables lateral movement of protein within the overall bilayer. This model was given by ________________ and ________________ in________________ .

24. Movement of water by diffusion across plasma membrane is called ________________ .

25. Na+/K+ pump is example of ________________ transport.

26. In cell wall of plant cell, ________________ wall is capable of growth and ________________ wall is formed on inner side of cell.

27. The middle lamella is a layer made up of ________________ pectate which glues neighbouring cells together and ________________ connect the cytoplasm of neighbouring cells.

28. The endomembrane system include cell organelles such as ________________ , ________________ and________________ .

29. The ER bearing ________________ on their surface is called RER.

30. The SER is the major site of synthesis of ________________ .

CHAPTER SEVENTEEN

Cell Cycle and Cell Division

According to the cell theory, cells arise from preexisting cells. The process by which this occurs is called cell division. Cell division is a very important process in all living organisms.

- During the division of a cell, DNA replication and cell growth also take place.
- All these processes, i.e., cell division, DNA replication, and cell growth, hence, have to take place in a coordinated way to ensure correct division and formation of progeny cells containing intact genomes.

Any sexually reproducing organism starts its life cycle from a single-celled zygote. Cell division does not stop with the formation of the mature organism but continues throughout its life cycle.

- The stages through which a cell passes from one division to the next is called the cell cycle. Cell cycle is divided into two phases called -

(i) Interphase – a period of preparation for cell division, and
(ii) Mitosis (M phase) – the actual period of cell division.
Interphase is further subdivided into G1, S and G2.

1. G1 phase is the period when the cell grows and carries out normal metabolism. Most of the organelle duplication also occurs during this phase.
2. S phase marks the phase of DNA replication and chromosome duplication.
3. G2 phase is the period of **cytoplasmic growth.**

•Chromosome condensation occurs during prophase. Simultaneously, the centrioles move to the opposite poles. The nuclear envelope and the nucleolus disappear and the spindle fibres start appearing. Metaphase is marked by the alignment of chromosomes at the equatorial plate. During anaphase the centromeres divide and the chromatids start moving towards the two opposite poles.

•Once the chromatids reach the two poles, the chromosomal elongation starts, nucleolus and the nuclear membrane reappear. This stage is called the telophase.

•Nuclear division is then followed by the cytoplasmic division and is called cytokinesis. Mitosis thus, is the equational division in which the chromosome number of the parent is conserved in the daughter cell.

•In contrast to mitosis, meiosis occurs in the diploid cells, which are destined to form gametes. It is called the reduction division since it reduces the chromosome number by half while making the gametes.

Mitosis is also divided into four stages namely prophase, metaphase, anaphase and telophase.

•A typical eukaryotic cell cycle is illustrated by human cells in culture. These cells divide once in approximately every 24 hours . However, this duration of cell cycle can vary from organism to organism and also from cell type to cell type.

•Yeast for example, can progress through the cell cycle in only about 90 minutes.

•The cell cycle is divided into two basic phases:

1. Interphase (most active stage)

2. **M Phase (Mitosis phase): Most dramatic phase:** The M Phase represents the phase when the **actual cell division** or mitosis occurs and the interphase represents the phase between two successive M phases.

•It is significant to note that in the 24 hour average duration of cell cycle of a human cell, cell division proper lasts for only about **an hour.**

•The interphase lasts more than 95% of the duration of cell cycle. The M Phase starts with the nuclear division, corresponding to the separation of daughter chromosomes (karyokinesis) and usually ends with division of cytoplasm (cytokinesis).

•The interphase, though called the resting phase, is the time during which the cell is preparing for division by undergoing both cell growth and DNA replication in an orderly manner. The interphase is divided into three further phases: G1 , S , G2.

•G1 phase corresponds to the interval between mitosis and initiation of DNA replication.

•During G1 phase the cell is metabolically active and continuously grows but does not replicate its DNA. The length of G1 is variable.

•S or synthesis phase marks the period during which DNA synthesis or replication takes place.

•During this time the amount of DNA per cell doubles. If the initial amount of DNA is denoted as 2C then it increases to 4C.

•However, there is no increase in the chromosome number; if the cell had diploid or 2n number of chromosomes at G1, even after S phase the number of chromosomes remains the same, i.e., 2n.

•In animal cells, during the S phase, DNA replication begins in the nucleus, and the centriole duplicates in the cytoplasm.

•During the G2 phase, proteins are synthesised in preparation for mitosis while cell growth continues. **Some cells in the adult animals do not appear to exhibit division (e.g., heart cells, Nerve cells)** and many other cells divide only occasionally, as needed to replace cells that have been lost because of injury or cell death.

•These cells that do not divide further exit G1 phase to enter an inactive stage called quiescent stage (G0) of the cell cycle.

•Cells in this stage remain metabolically active but no longer proliferate unless called on to do so depending on the requirement of the organism.

•In animals, mitotic cell division is only seen in the diploid somatic cells. Against this, the plants can show mitotic divisions in both haploid and diploid cells.

•M PHASE: Actual Cell division : This is **the most dramatic period** of the cell cycle, involving a major reorganisation of virtually all components of the cell.

•Since the number of chromosomes in the parent and progeny cells is the same, it is also called as equational division.

•Though for convenience mitosis has been divided into four stages of nuclear division, it is very essential to understand that cell division is a progressive process and very clear-cut lines cannot be drawn between various stages.

Mitosis is divided into the following four stages:1. Prophase 2. Metaphase 3. Anaphase 4. Telophase

Prophase : which is the first stage of mitosis follows the S and G2 phases of interphase.

•In the S and G2 phases the new DNA molecules formed are not distinct but interwined.

•Prophase is marked by the initiation of condensation of chromosomal material.

•The chromosomal material becomes untangled during the process of chromatin condensation .

•The centriole, which had undergone duplication during S phase of interphase, now begins to move towards opposite poles of the cell.

•The completion of prophase can thus be marked by the following characteristic events: 1. Chromosomal material condenses to form compact mitotic chromosomes. Chromosomes are seen to be composed of two chromatids attached together at the centromere. 2. Initiation of the assembly of mitotic spindle, the microtubules, the proteinaceous components of the cell cytoplasm help in the process.

•Cells at the end of prophase, when viewed under the microscope, do not show golgi complexes, endoplasmic reticulum, nucleolus and the nuclear envelope.

Metaphase: The complete disintegration of the nuclear envelope marks the start of the second phase of mitosis, hence the chromosomes are spread through the cytoplasm of the cell.

•By this stage, condensation of chromosomes is completed and they can be observed clearly under the microscope. This then, is the stage at which morphology of chromosomes is most easily studied. At this stage, metaphase chromosome is made up of two sister chromatids, which are held together by the centromere .

•Small disc-shaped structures at the surface of the centromeres are called kinetochores. These structures serve as the sites of attachment of spindle fibres (formed by the spindle fibres) to the chromosomes that are moved into position at the centre of the cell.

•Hence, the metaphase is characterised by all the chromosomes coming to lie at the equator with one chromatid of each chromosome connected by its kinetochore to spindle fibres from one pole and its sister chromatid connected by its kinetochore to spindle fibres from the opposite pole .

•The plane of alignment of the chromosomes at metaphase is referred to as the metaphase plate. The key features of metaphase are: Spindle fibres attach to kinetochores of chromosomes.

•Chromosomes are moved to spindle equator and get aligned along metaphase plate through spindle fibres to both poles.

Anaphase: At the onset of anaphase, each chromosome arranged at the metaphase plate is split simultaneously and the two daughter chromatids, now referred to as chromosomes of the future daughter nuclei, begin their migration towards the two opposite poles.

•As each chromosome moves away from the equatorial plate, the centromere of each chromosome is towards the pole and hence at the leading edge, with the arms of the chromosome trailing behind . Thus, anaphase stage is characterised by the following key events:

•1. Centromeres split and chromatids separate.2. Chromatids move to opposite poles. 3. To see the shape of chromosome , anaphase is the best.

Telophase : At the beginning of the final stage of mitosis, i.e., telophase, the chromosomes that have reached their respective poles decondense and lose their individuality. The individual chromosomes can no longer be seen and chromatin material tends to collect in a mass in the two poles.

•This is the stage which shows the following key events: 1. Chromosomes cluster at opposite spindle poles and their identity is lost as discrete elements. 2. Nuclear envelope assembles around the chromosome clusters. 3. Nucleolus, golgi complex and ER reform.

Cytokinesis: Mitosis accomplishes not only the segregation of duplicated chromosomes into daughter nuclei (karyokinesis), but the cell itself is divided into two daughter cells by a separate process called cytokinesis at the end of which cell division is complete .

•In an animal cell, this is achieved by the appearance of a furrow in the plasma membrane. The furrow gradually deepens and ultimately joins in the centre dividing the cell cytoplasm into two.

•Plant cells however, are enclosed by a relatively inextensible cell wall, thererfore they undergo cytokinesis by a different mechanism. In plant cells, wall formation starts in the centre of the cell and grows outward to meet the existing lateral walls.

•The formation of the new cell wall begins with the formation of a simple precursor, called the cell-plate that represents the middle lamella between the walls of two adjacent cells.

•At the time of cytoplasmic division, organelles like mitochondria and plastids get distributed between the two daughter cells.

•In some organisms **karyokinesis is not followed by cytokinesis as a result of which multinucleate condition arises leading to the formation of syncytium (e.g., liquid endosperm in coconut).**

Significance of Mitosis :

•Mitosis or the equational division is usually restricted to the diploid cells only.

•However, in some lower plants and in some social insects haploid cells also divide by mitosis. It is very essential to understand the significance of this division in the life of an organism.

•Are you aware of some examples where you have studied about haploid and diploid insects?

•Mitosis results in the production of diploid daughter cells with identical genetic complement usually. The growth of multicellular organisms is due to mitosis.

•Cell growth results in disturbing the ratio between the nucleus and the cytoplasm. It therefore becomes essential for the cell to divide to restore the nucleo-cytoplasmic ratio.

•A very significant contribution of mitosis is cell repair. The cells of the upper layer of the epidermis, cells of the lining of the gut, and blood cells are being constantly replaced.

•Mitotic divisions in the meristematic tissues – the apical and the lateral cambium, result in a continuous growth of plants throughout their life.

•**Number of mitotic divisions** required for formation of n number of cells is n-1.

•**Number of generations (n)of mitosis** for producing x cells is x = **2** n

MEIOSIS:

The production of offspring by sexual reproduction includes the fusion of two gametes, each with a complete haploid set of chromosomes.

•Gametes are formed from specialised diploid cells. This specialised kind of cell division that reduces the chromosome number by half results in the production of haploid daughter cells.

•This kind of division is called meiosis.

•Meiosis ensures the production of haploid phase in the life cycle of sexually reproducing organisms whereas fertilisation restores the diploid phase.

•We come across meiosis during gametogenesis in plants and animals. This leads to the formation of haploid gametes.

•The key features of meiosis are as follows: z Meiosis involves two sequential cycles of nuclear and cell division called meiosis I and meiosis II but only a single cycle of DNA replication. 1. Meiosis I is initiated after the parental chromosomes have replicated to produce identical sister chromatids at the S phase. 2. Meiosis involves pairing of homologous chromosomes and recombination between them. 3. Four haploid cells are formed at the end of meiosis II. Meiotic events can be grouped under the following phases:

Meiosis I Prophase I: Prophase of the first meiotic division is typically longer and more complex when compared to prophase of mitosis. It has been further subdivided into the following five phases based on chromosomal behaviour, i.e., Leptotene, Zygotene, Pachytene, Diplotene and Diakinesis. (LZPDD)

•**Leptotene:** During leptotene stage the chromosomes become gradually visible under the light microscope. The compaction of chromosomes continues throughout leptotene. This is followed by the second stage of prophase I called zygotene.

Zygotene: During this stage chromosomes start pairing together and this process of association is called **synapsis.** Such paired chromosomes are called homologous chromosomes. Electron micrographs of this stage indicate that chromosome synapsis is accompanied by the formation of complex structure called synaptonemal complex. The complex formed by a pair of synapsed homologous chromosomes is called a bivalent or a tetrad. However, these are more clearly visible at the next stage.

The first two stages of prophase I are relatively short-lived compared to the next stage that is pachytene.

Pachytene : During this stage bivalent chromosomes now clearly appears as **tetrads.** This stage is characterised by the appearance of recombination nodules, the sites at which crossing over occurs between non-sister chromatids of the homologous chromosomes.

•Crossing over is the exchange of genetic material between two homologous chromosomes.

•Crossing over is also an enzyme-mediated process and the enzyme involved is called **Recombinase.**

•Crossing over leads to recombination of genetic material on the two chromosomes.

•Recombination between homologous chromosomes is completed by the end of pachytene, leaving the chromosomes linked at the sites of crossing over.

Diplotene: The beginning of diplotene is recognised by **the dissolution of the synaptonemal complex** and the tendency of the recombined homologous chromosomes of the bivalents to separate from each other except at the sites of crossovers. These X-shaped structures, are called chiasmata.

•In oocytes of some vertebrates, diplotene can last for months or years. **(Dictyotene – suspended diplotene)**

Q. In oocycte of some vertebrates, a particular subdivision of meiotic cell division also called dictyotene stage which lasts for month or years. This particular sub-division is-

(1) Diplotene (2) Anaphase (3) Leptotene (4) Telophase

Diakinesis: The final stage of meiotic prophase I is diakinesis.

•This is marked by **terminalization of chiasmata.** During this phase the chromosomes are fully condensed and the meiotic spindle is assembled to prepare the homologous chromosomes for separation.

•By the end of diakinesis, the nucleolus disappears and the nuclear envelope also breaks down.

•Diakinesis represents transition to metaphase I.

Metaphase I: The bivalent chromosomes align on the equatorial plate .

•The microtubules from the opposite poles of the spindle attach to the pair of homologous chromosomes.

Anaphase I: The homologous chromosomes separate, while sister chromatids remain associated at their centromeres .

Telophase I: The nuclear membrane and nucleolus reappear, cytokinesis follows and this is called as **diad of cells** .

•Although in many cases the chromosomes do undergo some dispersion, they do not reach the extremely extended state of the interphase nucleus.

•The stage between the two meiotic divisions is called interkinesis and is generally short lived.

•Interkinesis is followed by prophase II, a much simpler prophase than prophase I.

Meiosis II

•**Prophase II:** Meiosis II is initiated immediately after cytokinesis, usually before the chromosomes have fully elongated. In contrast to meiosis I, meiosis II resembles a normal mitosis. The nuclear membrane disappears by the end of prophase II . The chromosomes again become compact.

•**Metaphase II:** At this stage the chromosomes align at the equator and the microtubules from opposite poles of the spindle get attached to the kinetochores of sister chromatids.

•**Anaphase II:** It begins with the simultaneous splitting of the centromere of each chromosome (which was holding the sister chromatids together), allowing them to move toward opposite poles of the cell .

•**Telophase II:** Meiosis ends with telophase II, in which the two groups of chromosomes once again get enclosed by a nuclear envelope; cytokinesis follows resulting in the formation of tetrad of cells i.e., four haploid daughter cells

•**SIGNIFICANCE OF MEIOSIS :** Meiosis is the mechanism by which conservation of specific chromosome number of each species is achieved across generations in sexually reproducing organisms, even though the process, per se, paradoxically, results in reduction of chromosome number by half.

•It also increases the genetic variability in the population of organisms from one generation to the next.

•Variations are very important for the process of evolution.

Q . 2n =68 chromosomes, then how many bivalents (tetrad) will be formed in meiosis- I- --> 34

•In sexual reproduction when the two gametes fuse the chromosome number is restored to the value in the parent. Meiosis is divided into two phases – meiosis I and meiosis II. In the first meiotic division the homologous chromosomes pair to form bivalents, and undergo crossing over.

•Meiosis I has a long prophase, which is divided further into five phases. These are leptotene, zygotene, pachytene, diplotene and diakinesis.

•During metaphase I the bivalents arrange on the equatorial plate.

•This is followed by anaphase I in which homologous chromosomes move to the opposite poles with both their chromatids.

•Each pole receives half the chromosome number of the parent cell.

•In telophase I, the nuclear membrane and nucleolus reappear. Meiosis II is similar to mitosis. During anaphase II the sister chromatids separate.

Thus at the end of meiosis four haploid cells are formed.

NCERT Home work :

1. Any sexually reproducing organism starts its life cycle from a single-celled ________________
2. The stages through which a cell passed from one division to the next is called ________________ .
3. Yeast progresses through the cell cycle in ________________ minute.
4. The cell cycle is divided into two phase ________________ and ________________ .
5. Nuclear division is known as ________________ while cytoplasm division is known as ________________ .
6. In cell cycle, the resting phase during which cell is preparing for cell division is called ________________ .
7. ________________ phase of interphase is period when cell grows and carries out normal metabolism.
8. During ________________ phase of interphase, amount of DNA per cell doubles.
9. If the cell has 2n number of chromosome at G1, then number of chromosome after S phase will be________________ .
10. G0 phase of cell cycle is called ________________ stage.
11. During ________________ phase of M-phase of cell cycle, duplicated centriole begins to move towards opposite pole of cell.
12. ________________ structure on surface of centromere serve as the sites of attachment of spindle fibres to the chromosome.
13. The plane of alignment of chromosome at metaphase is referred to as the ________________ .
14. ________________ stage of M-phase is characterised by splitting of centromeres and seperation of chromatids.
15. Nuclear envelope assembles around chromosome cluster in ________________ stage of M-phase.
16. During cytokinesis in plant cell, formation of cell plate occur that represent ________________ between the walls of two adjacent cells.
17. During ________________ stage of Prophase I, chromosome start pairing together. This process of association is called ________________ .
18. During zygotene sta ge, the complex formed by a pair of synapsed Homologous chromosome is called a ________________ .
19. Crossing over occur during ________________ stage of Prophase I and is enzyme-mediated process and enzyme involved is called ________________ .
20. The site of crossover is X-shaped strcuture called ________________ in diplotene stage.
21. Mitosis is also called ________________ whereas meiosis is called ________________ .
22. Number of daughter cell form after mitosis is ________________ and after meiosis is ________________ .
23. Crossing-over occurs between ________________ chromatids of homologous chromosome.
24. -----------------is a very important process in all living organisms. During the division of a cell, DNA replication and cell growth also take place. All these processes, i.e., cell division, DNA replication, and cell growth, hence, have to take place in a coordinated way to ensure correct division and formation of progeny cells containing intact genomes.
25. The sequence of events by which a cell duplicates its genome, synthesises the other constituents of the cell and eventually divides into two daughter cells is termed ----------------.
26. Although cell growth (in terms of cytoplasmic increase) is a -------------------process, DNA synthesis occurs only during one specific stage in the cell cycle.
27. The replicated chromosomes (DNA) are then distributed to daughter nuclei by a complex series of events during cell division. These events are themselves under -------------- control.
28. A typical eukaryotic cell cycle is illustrated by human cells in culture. These cells divide once in approximately every ------------ hours .
29. However, this duration of cell cycle can vary from organism to organism and also from cell type to cell type. --------------- for example, can progress through the cell cycle in only about 90 minutes.

30. The cell cycle is divided into two basic phases: 1 Interphase 2. ----------------------------Phase (Mitosis phase) The M Phase represents the phase when the actual cell division or mitosis occurs and the ----------------- represents the phase between two successive M phases.

31. It is significant to note that in the 24 hour average duration of cell cycle of a human cell, cell division proper lasts for only about ------------ hour.

32. The interphase lasts more than ----------------% of the duration of cell cycle. The M Phase starts with the nuclear division, corresponding to the separation of daughter chromosomes (karyokinesis) and usually ends with division of cytoplasm (------------------------).

33. The interphase, though called the -------------------phase, is the time during which the cell is preparing for division by undergoing both cell growth and DNA replication in an orderly manner. The interphase is divided into three further phases: G1 , ----------------- , G2

34. G1 phase corresponds to the interval between ----------------- and initiation of DNA replication.

35. During ------------ phase the cell is metabolically active and continuously grows but does not replicate its DNA.

36. ----------------- phase marks the period during which DNA synthesis or replication takes place.

37. During this time the amount of DNA per cell -----------------. If the initial amount of DNA is denoted as 2C then it increases to ----------------.

38. However, there is no increase in the chromosome ------------------; if the cell had diploid or 2n number of chromosomes at G1, even after S phase the number of chromosomes remains --------------------------, i.e., 2n.

39. In animal cells, during the S phase, DNA replication begins in the ------------, and the centriole duplicates in the --------------------.

40. During the G2 phase, proteins are synthesised in preparation for mitosis while cell growth continues. Some cells in the adult animals do not appear to exhibit division (e.g.,------------------cells) and many other cells divide only occasionally, as needed to replace cells that have been lost because of injury or cell death.

41. These cells that do not divide further exit G1 phase to enter an inactive stage called ------------------ stage (G0) of the cell cycle.

42. Cells in this stage remain metabolically active but no longer -------------------- unless called on to do so depending on the requirement of the organism.

43. In animals, --------------------- cell division is only seen in the diploid somatic cells. Against this, the plants can show mitotic divisions in both haploid and diploid cells.

44. -----------------This is the most dramatic period of the cell cycle, involving a major reorganisation of virtually all components of the cell.

45. Since the number of chromosomes in the parent and progeny cells is --------------, it is also called as equational division.

46. Though for convenience mitosis has been divided into four stages of nuclear division, it is very essential to understand that cell division is a ------------------process and very clear-cut lines cannot be drawn between various stages.

47. Mitosis is divided into the following four stages: 1. Prophase 2. --------------- 3. Anaphase 4. Telophase

48. ---------------- which is the first stage of mitosis follows the S and G2 phases of interphase.

49. In the S and ------------- phases the new DNA molecules formed are not distinct but interwined.

50. rophase is marked by the initiation of ---------------- of chromosomal material.

51. The chromosomal material becomes --------------------- during the process of chromatin condensation .

52. The -----------------------, which had undergone duplication during S phase of interphase, now begins to move towards opposite poles of the cell.

53. The completion of prophase can thus be marked by the following characteristic events: 1. Chromosomal material condenses to form compact mitotic chromosomes. Chromosomes are seen to be composed of --------------- chromatids attached together at the centromere. 2. Initiation of the assembly of mitotic ---------------, the microtubules, the proteinaceous components of the cell cytoplasm help in the process.

54. Cells at the end of ----------------------, when viewed under the microscope, do not show golgi complexes, endoplasmic reticulum, nucleolus and the nuclear envelope.

55. -------------------------- : The complete disintegration of the nuclear envelope marks the start of the second phase of mitosis, hence the chromosomes are spread through the cytoplasm of the cell. By this stage, condensation of chromosomes is --------------------and they can be observed clearly under the microscope. This then, is the stage at which morphology of chromosomes is most easily studied. At this stage, metaphase chromosome is made up of two sister chromatids, which are held together by the centromere .

56. Small disc-shaped structures at the surface of the centromeres are called -------------------. These structures serve as the sites of attachment of spindle fibres (formed by the spindle fibres) to the chromosomes that are moved into position at the centre of the cell.

57. Hence, the metaphase is characterised by all the chromosomes coming to lie at the ---------------------with one chromatid of each chromosome connected by its kinetochore to spindle fibres from one pole and its sister chromatid connected by its kinetochore to spindle fibres from the opposite pole .

58. The plane of alignment of the chromosomes at metaphase is referred to as the -----------------------------. The key features of metaphase are: z Spindle fibres attach to kinetochores of chromosomes. Chromosomes are moved to spindle equator and get aligned along metaphase plate through spindle fibres to both poles.

59. Anaphase : At the onset of anaphase, each chromosome arranged at the metaphase plate is-------------- simultaneously and the two daughter chromatids, now referred to as chromosomes of the future daughter nuclei, begin their migration towards the two opposite poles.

60. As each chromosome moves away from the equatorial plate, the -------------------of each chromosome is towards the pole and hence at the leading edge, with the arms of the chromosome trailing behind . Thus, anaphase stage is characterised by the following key events: 1. Centromeres split and ----------------- separate.2. Chromatids move to opposite poles.

61. Telophase: At the beginning of the ----------------- stage of mitosis, i.e., telophase, the chromosomes that have reached their respective poles -------------------- and lose their individuality.The individual chromosomes can no longer be seen and chromatin material tends to collect in a mass in the two poles.

62. This is the stage which shows the following key events: 1. Chromosomes cluster at opposite spindle poles and their identity is ------------------- as discrete elements. 2. Nuclear envelope assembles around the chromosome clusters. 3. ---------------------, golgi complex and ER reform.

63. Cytokinesis : Mitosis accomplishes not only the segregation of duplicated chromosomes into daughter nuclei (---------------------), but the cell itself is divided into two daughter cells by a separate process called cytokinesis at the end of which cell division is complete .

64. In an animal cell, this is achieved by the appearance of a --------------------- in the plasma membrane. The furrow gradually deepens and ultimately joins in the centre dividing the cell cytoplasm into two.

65. Plant cells however, are enclosed by a relatively inextensible cell wall, thererfore they undergo cytokinesis by a different mechanism. In plant cells, wall formation starts in the --------------------of the cell and grows outward to meet the existing lateral walls.

66. The formation of the new cell wall begins with the formation of a simple precursor, called the cell-plate that represents the ------------------- between the walls of two adjacent cells.

67. At the time of cytoplasmic division, organelles like -------------------------and plastids get distributed between the two daughter cells.

68. In some organisms karyokinesis is not followed by cytokinesis as a result of which multinucleate condition arises leading to the formation of -----------------(e.g., liquid endosperm in --------------).

69. Mitosis or the ---------------- division is usually restricted to the diploid cells only.

70. However, in some ----------------- plants and in some social insects haploid cells also divide by mitosis. It is very essential to understand the significance of this division in the life of an organism.

71. Are you aware of some examples where you have studied about haploid and diploid insects? Mitosis results in the production of ------------------ daughter cells with identical genetic complement usually.

72. The growth of multicellular organisms is due to ----------------.

73. Cell growth results in disturbing the ratio between the nucleus and the cytoplasm. It therefore becomes essential for the cell to divide to restore the nucleo- --------------- ratio.

74. A very significant contribution of mitosis is cell -------------------------.

75. The cells of the ---------------layer of the epidermis, cells of the lining of the gut, and blood cells are being constantly replaced.

76. Mitotic divisions in the meristematic tissues – the apical and the ------------------- cambium, result in a continuous growth of plants throughout their life.

77. The production of offspring by sexual reproduction includes the ------------------of two gametes, each with a complete haploid set of chromosomes.

78. Gametes are formed from specialised -------------------cells. This specialised kind of cell division that reduces the chromosome number by half results in the production of haploid daughter cells. This kind of division is called -----------------.

79. Meiosis ensures the production of haploid phase in the life cycle of sexually reproducing organisms whereas --------------- restores the diploid phase.

80. We come across meiosis during ------------------------- in plants and animals. This leads to the formation of haploid gametes.

81. The key features of meiosis are as follows: 1. Meiosis involves two sequential cycles of nuclear and cell division called meiosis I and meiosis II but only a single cycle of DNA----------------- 1. Meiosis I is initiated after the parental chromosomes have replicated to produce identical sister chromatids at the ------------------phase. 2. Meiosis involves pairing of homologous chromosomes and ---------------------- between them. 3. -------------------- haploid cells are formed at the end of meiosis II.

82. Meiosis I Prophase I: Prophase of the first meiotic division is typically ------------------- and more complex when compared to prophase of mitosis.

83. It has been further subdivided into the following five phases based on chromosomal -----------------------, i.e., Leptotene, Zygotene, Pachytene, Diplotene and Diakinesis.

84. During leptotene stage the chromosomes become gradually visible under the light microscope. The compaction of chromosomes continues throughout leptotene. This is followed by the second stage of prophase I called ----------------------.

85. During this (--------------------) stage chromosomes start pairing together and this process of association is called -------------------. Such paired chromosomes are called homologous chromosomes.

86. Electron micrographs of this stage indicate that chromosome synapsis is accompanied by the formation of complex structure called -------------------------------

87. The complex formed by a pair of synapsed homologous chromosomes is called a bivalent or a ---------------. However, these are more clearly visible at the next stage.

88. The first two stages of prophase I are relatively -----------------s-lived compared to the next stage that is pachytene.

89. During this stage bivalent chromosomes now clearly appears as tetrads. This stage is characterised by the appearance of recombination nodules, the sites at which crossing over occurs between non-sister chromatids of the --------------------------- chromosomes.

90. ---------------------------- is the exchange of genetic material between two homologous chromosomes.

91. Crossing over is also an enzyme-mediated process and the enzyme involved is called ------------------.

92. Crossing over leads to recombination of genetic material on the two chromosomes. Recombination between homologous chromosomes is completed by the end of -------------------, leaving the chromosomes linked at the sites of crossing over.

93. The beginning of diplotene is recognised by the dissolution of the synaptonemal complex and the tendency of the recombined homologous chromosomes of the bivalents to separate from each other except at the sites of crossovers. These X-shaped structures, are called---------------------.

94. In oocytes of some vertebrates, ------------------------------- can last for months or years.

95. The final stage of meiotic prophase I is ---------------------.

96. This is marked by -------------------of chiasmata. During this phase the chromosomes are fully condensed and the meiotic spindle is assembled to prepare the homologous chromosomes for separation.

97. By the end of ------------------------, the nucleolus disappears and the nuclear envelope also breaks down.

98. Diakinesis represents transition to ---------------------.

99. Metaphase I: The ---------------------------chromosomes align on the equatorial plate .

100. The -------------------------- from the opposite poles of the spindle attach to the pair of homologous chromosomes.

101. ------------------------: The homologous chromosomes separate, while sister chromatids remain associated at their centromeres .

102. ------------------: The nuclear membrane and nucleolus reappear, cytokinesis follows and this is called as diad of cells .

103. Although in many cases the chromosomes do undergo some --------------------------, they do not reach the extremely extended state of the interphase nucleus.

104. The stage between the two meiotic divisions is called ---------------------and is generally short lived.

105. ------------------is followed by prophase II, a much simpler prophase than prophase I.

106. Meiosis II Prophase II: Meiosis II is initiated immediately after--------------------, usually before the chromosomes have fully elongated.

107. In contrast to meiosis I, meiosis II resembles a normal -----------------------. The nuclear membrane disappears by the end of prophase II .

108. The chromosomes again become --------------------------------.

109. Metaphase II: At this stage the chromosomes align at the ----------------- and the microtubules from opposite poles of the spindle get attached to the kinetochores of sister chromatids.

110. Anaphase II: It begins with the simultaneous ------------------ of the centromere of each chromosome (which was holding the sister chromatids together), allowing them to move toward opposite poles of the cell .

111. Telophase II: Meiosis ends with telophase II, in which the two groups of chromosomes once again get enclosed by a ---------------------; cytokinesis follows resulting in the formation of tetrad of cells i.e., ---------------------------- haploid daughter cells .

112. Meiosis is the mechanism by which conservation of specific chromosome number of each species is achieved across generations in --------------------- reproducing organisms, even though the process, per se, paradoxically, results in reduction of chromosome number by half. It also increases the genetic variability in the population of organisms from one generation to the next. Variations are very important for the process of -------------------.

Printed by Libri Plureos GmbH in Hamburg,
Germany